CW00642529

Patches
of
Heaven

Second revised edition

Alex. I. Askaroff

Other titles by the same author

Random Threads Volume I
Patches of Heaven
ISBN 0-9539410-4-3
(Former ISBN 0-9539410-1-9)

Random Threads Volume II
Skylark Country
ISBN 0-9539410-2-7

Random Threads Volume III
High Streets & Hedgerows
ISBN 0-9539410-3-5

Books published containing the author's work

A Celebration of Childhood, Rivacre Paperback
Natural Peace, Anchor Books Paperback
Poetry of Kent, Millfield Paperback
This Natural World, Arrival Press Hardback
South East Poets, Arrival Press Hardback
Let's do Lunch, Remus new fiction Paperback
Anchor Poets, Anchor Books Hardback
This Vanishing World, Poetry Now Hardback
Web of Thoughts, Anchor Books Hardback
The Good Ol' Days, Arrival Press Hardback
New Rhymes for Children, Arrival Press Hardback
A Tapestry of Thoughts , Spotlight Paperback
Mixed Musings , Poetry Now Hardback
Special Occasions, Arrival Press Hardback

Works in progress:
Nooks & Crannies of East Sussex
The Summer Fayre

Cover photographs: By Sarah Askaroff
Front cover, The River Cuckmere, one of England's finest meandering rivers.
Back cover, Eastbourne from Whitbread Hollow with Pinnacle Point,
(The Sugar Loaf) just visible in the foreground. It was called Sugar Loaf in Victorian
times as it resembled the large lumps of sugar delivered to the household.

RANDOM THREADS
Volume 1

Patches
of
Heaven

Second revised edition

By
Alex. I. Askaroff
© 2001
Email: alexsussex@aol.com
www.sussexsewingmachines.com
www.crowsnestpublications.com

CROWS NEST PUBLICATIONS
148 WILLINGDON PARK DRIVE
EASTBOURNE
EAST SUSSEX
ENGLAND
BN22 0DG

Copyright © by Crows Nest Publications 2001

SECOND REVISED EDITION
FIRST EDITION 2001
SECOND EDITION 2003

PAPERBACK ISBN
0-9539410-4-3

CIP information library reference
NOSTALGIA

Printed by
Tansleys the Printers
Seaford
East Sussex

For more information on how to order this book visit our websites @

http://www.sussexsewingmachines.com
http://crowsnestpublications.com

Introduction

In the Victorian era many an intrepid traveller would set off, notebook in hand and travel. They would move around the country describing the places and people they met, the local accents and countryside they saw. Then once home they would put all their experiences down on paper and publish.

My books are really a modern version of those travels. Unlike William Cobbett and his rural rides, my trusty steed is a Land Rover which over many years has never let me down. Together we have travelled the highways and byways of my beloved county. We have visited homes and farms up dusty trails, and unseen paths meandering through some of the most glorious places on this planet.

During my daily work I have met old Sussex folk that time has forgotten and rambled along my way taking notes as I went. Here is the start of my travels.

Alex I Askaroff

You can see my technical editor 'Zippy' carefully pointing out a paragraph that needs work.

CONTENTS

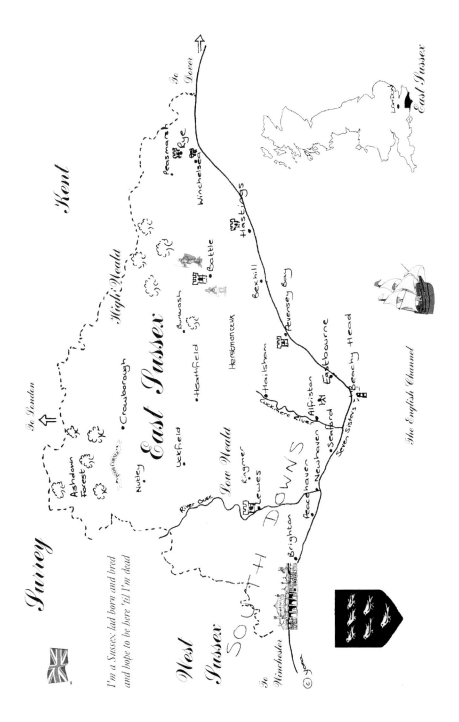

Surrey

Kent

West Sussex

East Sussex

*I'm a Sussex lad born and bred
and hope to be here 'til I'm dead*

High Weald

Low Weald

SOUTH DOWNS

East Sussex

To London

To Dover

To Winchester

Ashdown Forest

Crowborough

Nutley

Uckfield

Ringmer

Lewes

River Ouse

Brighton

Peacehaven

Newhaven

Seaford

Seven Sisters

Beachy Head

Eastbourne

Alfriston

Hailsham

Heathfield

Burwash

Battle

Heathmonceux

Bexhill

Pevensey Bay

Hastings

Winchelsea

Rye

Peasmarsh

The English Channel

East Sussex

London

© Jana

Author's Note

I must point out a little thing worth mentioning at the start of this book.

Although I love writing stories as many of my old English teachers will tell you I am no literary master. I thought a semicolon was part of your stomach and the best thing to do with verbs is sprinkle them on your Sunday roast. I am sure my teachers would be pleasantly surprised if not astounded at my decision to write down my travels. Their efforts to get the school lout to finish his homework in time has paid off – if a little late in life.

I sometimes write so much so fast that my fingers hurt and my brain aches. My grammar on a good day is OK.

On a bad day – well don't ask.

This amateur production has been a labour of love not an academic triumph.

Without the enthusiasm and support from so many of my family and friends it would never have got started. Enjoy it in the same spirit that it has been written.

Revised note: *You can imagine my amazement when by word of mouth alone, no publishers or agents, no bookshops or publicity, the books sold so fast that we needed to reprint. They have gone to the four corners of the world from Alaska to Australia.*

Email: alexsussex@aol.com

For Yana, Sarah and Tom

Acknowledgments

Many people have made this book possible. There is the endless encouragement from so many readers on the Internet. Ralph, who read the finished manuscript and pointed out many corrections and Stevie, who sat down and ploughed through the grammar. I know how difficult that was and so many thanks Stevie for spending a hard week's work on this book. Also a huge thank-you to Lin Hall who has helped to edit this revised edition.

I want to thank Yana. I first met Yana when I was 11. We shared a class together for two years, however it was not until we met again at college that I fell in love.

Yana, you are my strength, my rock and the very air that I breathe. You are my support when I fail, and wise when I am not. We all want to believe in miracles. Because of you every day is a miracle.

Prologue

How It All Started

Well where do you start your first book? From the beginning I suppose, so hang on to your hats, here we go!

I was born into the sewing world in the late 1950s. My Mum was out buying fish from Bob Clarke the fishmonger when she realised that I was coming into the world. She shouted to Bob for help. He promptly picked up his cart and bolted off-down Eversfield Road as fast as his little fat legs could carry him!

My Mum managed to get inside to the settee and out I popped. Bob always used to laugh about the way he panicked. We still bought fish from him so Mumsie could not have been too upset.

I was the number-three of six boys and the family was growing fast. My parents had a vast factory down one end of Willowfield Road in the small seaside town of Eastbourne on the south coast of England. To a child the factory seemed endless. It was around 20 to 30 thousand square feet in area (about 2500 m) and that was before we bought an even bigger factory next door and joined the two.

My parents were business people so, along with my six brothers, we were part of the business too. By the age of two I was already modelling for company brochures and by five I was whisked up to the great city of London for photo shoots.

The first time I was on the train to London I stared boggle-eyed out of the carriage windows at the endless rows of houses. I knew that there were lots of people in the world, now I had found out where they all lived.

Our factory had huge cutting-room tables which was handy for changing my nappy. Automatic machines ran up and down them all day laying up miles of fabric. Then the cutters would slice the precious cloth into a hundred different patterns.

One cutter, Pepe, an Italian who always made me laugh had cut several of his fingers off over the years. His left hand was a series of different length stumps. One day he got fed up with England and went back to his homeland. He said to me that he wanted to keep his last few fingers. I heard sometime later that he had sliced another one off!

Ronnie was another cutter. He had flame red hair and a temper to match, although he was a small man when his blood was up he would stand up to a six foot six lorry driver and give him a tongue lashing that would make a drunken navvy cringe.

My favourite of the cutters and good friend was Cyril Johnson, he would work all day and go home smiling. He never upset a single person and was so skilled at his job that he made a difficult cut-out look simple. Even now at over 70 he is still in such demand that he cannot retire.

As kids we ran amok in the factory. Crawling under sewing machines playing with the endless supply of cardboard rolls that the fabric came on. They made the best swords in the world. Each one was carefully selected for weight and balance, from the box behind the cutting room door, before bloody combat ensued in the yard.

Beginnings

My mother was a skilled Viennese seamstress and had a wonderful design ability too. She invented such things as the Raincape that simply pulled over a pushchair to keep the baby dry in the rain. Also other things like the Top'n'Tail, a changing-mat that baby could not roll off, with pouches at the bottom for things such as talc and nappy-rash cream.

My dad was born in Moscow at the start of the Russian revolution in 1917. He was smuggled out of the country as a child. Some 30 years later, and two lifetimes of experiences, he settled in Eastbourne. Igor, you can't get a more Russian name than that, was able to sell anything. He was the most natural businessman I have ever met. By the time I knew him he was a success but during his long struggle he had done everything from selling ice cream to working as a barman. He sat behind his large leather-topped desk signing papers and arranging deals before gliding off in his huge Jaguar.

The stair-well walls leading to the offices were lined with patent documents for many great ideas. Ideas that were produced in their thousands every week and went to the four corners of the world – from New Zealand to Iceland. We were supplying film stars and royalty alike. Harrods would place special orders for special people and even more special babies.

For over 30 years the names Simplantex and Premiere Baby were synonymous in Britain with the best you could buy for your baby. We would catch glimpses of babies wrapped in our products being carried around by the rich and famous and on TV.

Growing up in such an environment, surrounded by continuous manufacturing and the hum of sewing machines, it was only natural that I became interested in machinery.

In our cellar at 7 Ashburnham Gardens stood a dilapidated old Singer treadle machine. On several occasions when I had been a monster, like the time I threw a stone straight through my parent's plate glass mirror, I had the pleasure of incarceration with the Singer.

It had not been all my fault. Nick, my elder brother, had wound me up like a top before I had launched the stone directly at him. I had no thought of the mirror behind. No thought, that was, until he ducked!

It went through the plate-glass like a bullet. The mirror had stretched from the floor to the ceiling. It all happened in slow motion. Even Nick running away laughing.

Had he planned the whole affair? I often wonder. He was far too smart for the rest of us.

So, I was back in the cellar with the old Singer. I often wondered what devious deed the machine had done to deserve life imprisonment down in the dark depths of 7 Ashburnham Gardens. It turned out to be Mumsie's first sewing machine with which she started the business.

Many years later I dragged that old machine out of the dungeon, like the Count of Monte Cristo, had it serviced and polished and brought it back to working condition. I placed it in the main hall at the factory for all our visitors to see. What a splendid sight that machine was and the topic of many a conversation.

As time rolled on and I grew up I undertook a four-year engineering course and, after several jobs, started in the family business. At the factory I had the best engineers teach me more about the sewing machines.

David, who ran the local sewing shop in Seaside, took me under his wing and led me through the minefield of industrial sewing machines. Simon, who was the head engineer at Jaeger spent his Saturdays training me further. Even good old Uncle Gordon, whose family had sewing machine shops almost from Victorian times, taught me secrets so dearly guarded in the trade.

Eventually the skill that I now have was ingrained into me. I became one with the sewing machine. I could walk across rice-paper with no trace! Whoops, there I go, getting carried away. Truthfully, I will be forever in their debt. Learning the trade was not without its dangers. For example, Simon who I am sure won't mind me saying, had a nasty scrape while teaching me repairs.

It was a Saturday morning and he was teaching me the basics about the feed on a Brother industrial. This is a most important adjustment on a high-speed machine. A bit like the tyres on a car. The whole performance of a machine sewing over 5,000 stitches a minute depends on a good feed mechanism.

Well, we laid the head of the machine back onto its rest-peg so we could work underneath it. I said to Simon to be careful because I had noticed that the machine had no hinges securing the head to the table. It was like putting your head into a crocodile's mouth.

Well you can guess what happened. A few minutes into the tricky operation, while Simon's head was right inside the machine, the sewing machine slipped and pinned Simon's head to the table.

Wow! I knew it hurt. I was cringing like when you see something horrible on TV but also laughing hysterically at the comic situation.

It took a few seconds of watching Simon desperately trying to reach round his head to push the Brother machine off before I sprang to his aid. He had a nasty cut and his glasses were broken but, being a true professional, he carried on with the operation. Those were the days! Young and innocent. I learnt from his mistake and to this day have never repeated it.

Back to work

I was the first of the six boys to start in the factory. I worked downstairs with the cutters. Dad was always off to a business meeting here or there. Eventually, after he retired, my mother had a go at running the business.

By now Nick and my younger brother Sam had joined the firm. Nick's influence was explosive. The company that had spent three decades growing to around a quarter of a million annual turnover suddenly started to expand at an amazing rate. The sewing machines that most summers were lent out to other factories such as Jarvis Leather Goods were soon being used non-stop.

The long holidays we used to have, due to lack of orders, soon disappeared and the ever-increasing workload meant all work and no play. Nick turned our seasonal business into a powerhouse of manufacturing. For a businessman this is paradise. Nick, like our Dad, was a natural businessman. Phone him at 3 am and talk to him about business and he is happy.

I, on the other hand, did not take to it so well. My fishing trips came less and less while my working hours went up and up.

Within a few years, under Nick's influence, the firm was exceeding two million pounds a year turnover and, remember, this was back in the eighties.

Mum took the opportunity to retire and the rest of us just put our heads down and worked, worked, worked. The company or, by now companies, were like monsters that had to be constantly fed. I felt like the little sparrow that had to feed a cuckoo in its nest. There was no stopping, no rest, just work. In each five-day period we had to manufacture £40,000 of goods just to break even.

Think about it. On Monday we would start the machines to lay and cut. By Friday thousands of items in hundreds of different shapes had to be sewn together, checked, packed and shipped. We imported the best raw materials from around the world. Corduroy from China, lace from Switzerland, woven fabric from Austria, hand-made palm-leaf baskets from Africa. Everything we needed to make our goods. Our price list contained over two thousand items.

We organised shows in London, and around the country, where we would show off our latest products. Things like Beatrix Potter soft toys or the latest musical potty that played a tune when you tinkled. I never did understand why that did not catch on, it worked brilliantly on my kids, you could not get them off the potty!

Maybe that was the problem?

Come to think of it, by now there could be adults all over the planet that would only pee to music.

We mingled with the very top of our trade. Lunches with Maclaren, the millionaire inventor of the baby buggy, visits to Nottingham lace factories where machines that had made lace for over a century thundered out new reels of lace for some of our products. We toured the famous Silver Cross pushchair factory where they were still hand-building the Rolls Royce of pushchairs. I watched with quiet admiration as an old man ran a perfect blue stripe along the carriage of a new pushchair earmarked for a young prince of the realm. He had been painting the same stripe for 30 years with a long sable brush. A true craftsman.

Money was flowing, business was fantastic, we were top of the heap. Gradually however, things that used to give me great pleasure seemed no longer important. Things like having a suit tailor-made by a Saville Row tailor and having three fittings to get it just perfect. Or being announced at the Ritz.

Staying in hotels like St Ermins, where a steak would cost a day's wages. St Ermins, a superb hotel, was the unofficial meeting place for spies, just around the block from MI5 and the base for allied intelligence during WWII. Our parties were the envy of the trade shows. I remember the company splashing out £10,000 on one night of partying.

We booked the entire top floor of the Kensington Roof Gardens in London. What a place it was, with flamingos wandering around beside the fountains. In the Swinging Sixties it used to be the Biba Centre, a huge boutique store selling such makes as Mary Quant. Along with Petticoat Lane, the Biba Centre was the hottest place in town. Stars that were about to burst onto the fashion scene, like Twiggy, would rush down there to spend their hard-earned cash.

On our evening the men were all dressed in dinner suits, the women in ball gowns draped in their finest jewels. A live band serenaded us throughout the night.

They were super times but the pressure of work for me was mounting. I was like the stoker on an old steam train. Back when the train was quiet it was good fun. Now I was stoking the boiler non-stop. More coal, faster, faster, faster. I became a slave to that boiler and the more I shovelled the more the monster wanted.

It was around this time that I made what was to me, an amazing observation. My life was disappearing.

Let me try to explain. Ten years or more had passed in a blur. I had eaten, slept and even dreamt about work. It was an all-consuming passion. A thousand deadlines on a thousand products. I was aware that during a conversation with other people I did not know anything about the most basic goings on, for example local gossip.

What was happening outside of my immediate circle became irrelevant. I was unable to measure time. Most weeks, or months, even years, were the same. Rush, rush, rush.

It hit me like a ton of bricks. It was like the period at dawn when you have not quite woken. You look at the clock and it says 6 am, you glance again only seconds later and it reads 6.30. I could not distinguish much about any month or any year. Work was silently and efficiently stealing my life.

This is how you can understand it. It is not Einstein's Theory but, to me, far more important. Imagine you are in a racing car speeding around a track. The track is life. You see very little, except the track immediately ahead. A moment's diversion leads to disaster. Like the time when, in my rush, I dropped ten rolls of Viennese lace into a bag needing Swiss broderie anglaise material. No problem, that is, until you see the result. Hundreds of cream cot quilts were sewn up with peach lace. They looked awful and had to be sold off cheap.

A single second's mistake that cost us thousands. These mistakes only occurred when concentration slacked. So, no slacking!

Now imagine if you got out of the racing car and got into a normal car and just doodled around the track of life. Suddenly you can notice things. Now get out of the car and get on a bike. You feel the wind in your hair. You notice the birds twittering and see other people.

Well, I wanted to jump out of the racing car and bloody-well walk. I could not stop time but I knew I could slow it down to a normal pace.

Second thoughts

I wanted to smell the grass and touch the flowers. To make idle chat with people that I didn't know. I did not want to be able to tell the time, almost down to the minute, by the sound of the factory. I wanted to stop my children's childhood disappearing through my fingers like grains of fine sand.

So there I was the engine-stoker on an old train that had grown beyond anyone's imagination. Nick on the other hand wanted more. He had decided that the firm was just not big enough. He started a chain of Premiere Baby shops to be franchised across the country. Another factory making toys down in the West Country. More, more, more.

One day after a huge show at Earls Court I looked at my children and thought enough was enough! I had missed so many important things.

That day I had arrived back from London just before midnight and there I was unlocking the factory gates before 6.30 the next morning. I had to plan my escape or my life was going to disappear. One day I would be asked into the office, patted on the back, handed a gold watch and told to retire!

Giving it up was not going to be easy. There were two problems. The so-called good life traps you with tempting chains of gold and you cannot take out an integral part of a mechanism and hope it will still work. As an engineer I was well aware of the stormy waters that I would have to get through to reach the safety of shore. Money, big houses and fast cars surrounded me. All were going to be lost if I jumped ship. The Rolls Royces and BMWs would have to be exchanged for a van with a tool kit. The paid holidays and pension would be lost. The champagne life would have to go if I was to be able to slow down and smell the roses.

It would be a great leap. I suppose a leap of faith. I was going from the security of a business that had never failed into the unknown. Away from a business that had clothed and supported me for so long. The only person I would have to blame for failure would be myself.

Each day, at the factory, I had the responsibility for around a hundred people. This would change to be just one person, me. The problem with dramatic changes, where you go from a lucrative life to a simple one, is that I had made no provision for it. Had my revelation of time hit me sooner in life I could have prepared for it!

So here I was, on the engine platform of the family steam-train, hanging on like grim death looking out into the dark abyss that was my future. Certain in the knowledge that I had to make the jump but with no idea of what lay in my path.

Coincidentally, just before I jumped, Nick had left for greener pastures. Whereas I wanted to slow down he wanted to build his empire unhindered by petty family politics. So he did.

As the time drew near I sold my shares to my younger brother Sam. After massive taxation because of my high tax bracket I was left with just enough money to settle my debts and buy my van and tools.

On the final day I parked the BMW in the factory yard, bade a few goodbyes and walked down the long drive to the factory gate. As I passed the gate I stopped and looked at the lock that I had unlocked so many times for so many years. I took a final glance at the factory too. I knew I would never be back.

The yard where I had played as a child, where my friends and I had played football, where I had parked my first car, the views that were so familiar, were all to be no more. The great times, like when the factory girls and an even more enthusiastic boy thought they might like to strip me naked before Christmas lunch, were all now in my memory. That time, after a frantic chase, I had had to dive out of a back window like a rabbit down a hole with my clothes hanging about my person in bits.

There was the memory of all the workers making Father Christmas outfits for the annual lunch. The sight of a hundred red and white costumes racing up the road to the restaurant is something that I will never forget.

The three-mile walk home from the factory was a short one. I was carried on wings of air. Subconsciously I knew I had made the right decision. I knew that my life was going to change in a million ways but they would be the right ways. Nick and I had left the family business that had grown for four decades in the safe hands of our four other brothers. Well, we thought we had….The business spiralled downhill faster than a pheasant full of buckshot. But, that's another story.

Disentanglement

The next few months were the trickiest. Estranged from my family that I had been with for over 30 years. They had taken the leaving of the family firm as an intolerable insult. Funnily, I thought I would miss them but the acrimonious meetings and backstabbing was something that I found I could happily live without.

Power, money and big families. What a mixture! I had left them all behind squabbling like children over the last cake at a party. I was so relieved. I felt like Caesar who had somehow cheated death on his way to the Senate and then escaped from Rome and was living in a retirement flat in Eastbourne.

Things went well until, completely out of the blue, a huge tax bill hit me. It was for rollover-tax due from money paid to Directors in years past. This tax was something that I knew nothing about and certainly for money that I had never had, but I was apparently liable.

I went to see my accountant. He looked through the details and sent me to a solicitor. There was no getting out of it. Pay the tax or prove I never had the money. Easier said than done. The thought of doing battle with the Family was a nightmare. It would open a real can of worms.

To pay or not to pay? That was the question.

It was a dilemma with no easy answer. I decided to pay the bill. It was crippling. The money that was to see me through the hardest months at the beginning of my venture, my safety net, was gone.

One of my friends, Eddy Graves, whose children I had babysat many years before was in the car trade. He found me a lovely little Renault van and let me have it at a price that I could afford. I bolted some extra car seats in the back for the kids and off we went.

Having no money at all makes you keen. I chased every penny that was available. I would travel far and wide fixing machines and sharpening scissors well into the night. I had to build up a customer base for repeat business. Although I had many contacts and plenty of suppliers I knew that I had to get the businesses in my area.

Luckily many fantastic friends gave me endless support and my wonderful wife, Yana, who had stood by me through the good times and bad, was my rock.

I had slid from the top of the ladder to the bottom without hitting anything in-between. When the money was not enough to cover our week's expenses Yana would do boot sales on the weekend – a bit like garage sales in America but on a larger scale. She would sell things that we could spare or do without. I knew things were really bad when I cut up the four-poster bed and made a table using the posts as the legs. I sold that and many other things to get us by.

The kettle was fibre-glassed up when it leaked and the kid's clothes lasted as long as they could be patched. In the winter we piled on three jumpers rather than turn the heating on.

Besides my home, and a few sewing machines that I had collected for years, I had one other possession that was dear to me, my 1966 Daimler car. I had lovingly restored it over many years and it was the last valuable thing that we had that could be sold. I had rebuilt her from a rusty shell to a beautiful, near pristine condition, work of art. In a depressed mood I booked her in at the local auction rooms and dreaded the trip.

However fate played another hand. Yana, who was coming back from a shopping trip, misjudged the garage wall. She hit the front of the Daimler, scraping the wing against the wooden door. Well now, most people would have stopped but, in a very feminine way, she decided that as she had gone so far and she might as well continue into the garage.

The result was that she scraped the car along its entire length, from the front bumper to the rear. The damage meant that the car had to be resprayed. During the weeks that this took our fortunes changed. Money from the schools and factories had started to roll in and for the first time we had money in the bank. Therefore the Daimler was safe. I could not afford to pay the road tax or even insure it any longer but it looked great in the garage. Now, years later, it is back on the road restored to her full glory.

Things were still tricky. As I called on customer after customer I had to learn how to deal with complete strangers in a friendly manner. This was so important because I was meeting them in their homes and fixing their machines. No more shouting out orders across the factory floor.

Now, all these years later, I almost feel as if I know the person before they open the door. This may be because we all fall into very similar patterns. As humans we are all individuals but we have a thousand similarities. Eventually I became totally at ease with people. One of the secrets of success.

Looking good

After the third year of running Sussex Sewing Machines we had our first holiday. One of my very close friends from school days, Andy Russell, lent us his car and we had a relaxing week driving around England. What a fantastic holiday that was. So special because it meant we had done it.

We had started our own business and survived. The future was looking good.

As the business grew, and with it our prosperity, the thing that I had dreamed of most was coming true. I was getting enough time to smell the roses. I would spend time chatting to strangers that would become friends.

During my travels I came across people that had wonderful stories to tell and I was ready to listen. I also had time to play with my kids before they went to school and help them with homework after school. Well, try to anyway.

Now, in a new millennium, my business is responsible for millions of pounds of machinery and around 7,000 customers in our area. I look after anyone and everyone with a sewing machine: schools, laundries, hospitals, hotels, factories and homes.

It seems like another life back at the family firm when dozens of women on piecework and bonuses were screaming for their machines to be fixed. I had left the monster behind and lived to tell the tale. Unfortunately, in Nick's and my absence, the monster had rolled over and died. A sad fate for what had been a superb business.

Déjà vu

One day, many years later, I had a call from the new owners that had bought the family giant. When I arrived at the factory what a shock it was. The day I had left the factory it was a heaving mass of humanity. They had a full order book and the future was bright. The good thing about babies is that there are always new ones coming along. The miner's strikes in the 1970s that caused the blackouts during the evenings led to one of the first baby booms. No TV meant everyone was getting up to something else!

When I had left, everywhere you looked there was noise and commotion, cutters, sewers, checkers, packers and office staff running here and there chasing orders.

I parked in the yard that I had not been back to for nearly a decade. It was empty save for one flashy sports car. The cutting rooms lay silent where cutting machines had ploughed the room all day. The sewing rooms, where there used to be so much noise you could not hear yourself think, had just a handful of machines left. They looked so sorry for themselves all alone.

I was on a ghost ship. The silence was dreadful. It was as if they had all perished. The canteen where we sat and had so many laughs as we swapped tales and jokes over a sandwich and drink was the saddest place of all. I felt a lump in my throat as I walked around. No one had come to greet me. I wandered – lonely and thoughtful.

The rooms where we used to hide as children were full of dusty junk. I walked about, stopping to look at the place where there was a hole in the floor. At the tender age of twenty I was rushing through the factory with a new Brother industrial machine. The wheels of the trolley hit a lump in the floor and tipped. In slow motion the machine rolled off the end of its table. As the heavy industrial head hit the floor it was like a cannon exploding.

In a split second a busy factory fell silent. Every eye was on me. All the machinists looked up from their machines. The packers and checkers all stopped. There was the sound of the cutters running up the stairs to get a look, then silence: complete and utter silence.

Suddenly a huge round of applause and whooping and shouting erupted spontaneously from everyone. The boss's son had made a big booboo. I turned a bright shade of pink, picked the machine up, bowed to my audience and trundled off with it as fast as my legs could go.

Times like those were brought back to me as I stood on the deck of my ghost ship. I felt tears well up in my eyes and had to look up and cough to clear my throat as one of the new owners walked towards me. He had no idea of the connection I felt to the old place. He just wanted to know if I was interested in the last few machines that they were getting rid of. I bought them and left. It was a sad day.

A new beginning

Luckily my youngest brother had listened to me before I left and split part of the business away from the parent company. This firm is still going strong so a part of the original has survived. Who knows, one day it may grow as large as the firm that it broke away from?

To begin with, in the early years of my business, many of the local factories were suspicious of me entering their premises. Whilst they were desperate to have someone with my ability to tune a machine they were also aware that with a lifetimes knowledge in manufacturing I could make almost anything I saw.

One factory was so cautious that they took the precaution of shielding their entire production from me. As I entered the factory I was guided along the corridors to the machines that needed work. Each door that could be closed was closed. Every opening was blocked with sheets or boxes so that I could see nothing.

Now, years later, we laugh about those precautions. I roam about with a free hand, often being given the keys to be able to start early.

As I travelled around my southeast corner of England I became more aware of its beauty. There were places that I had passed a million times and never noticed. Once I was off the beaten track I would be transported in time. Back to an England that only survives in books – or so I thought. Places like Ashdown Forest, the home of 100-acre Wood, where Winnie-the-Pooh came to life. The same forest where Henry VIII hunted deer.

Eastbourne is just the most perfect Victorian seaside town. It was designed and built by people with vision in an era of elegance. I have loved it and wandered around it since childhood. I saw it grow into the bustling holiday resort it is today.

I was born in a small corner of the United Kingdom, a tiny part of the world that had built the greatest empire our planet had ever seen. What had made this possible was the people that lived here. Their vision, character and often-bloody, history had made our country. Each day I would visit descendants of those people. Everyday people, people that grow from a soil so rich and a history so full.

Through these people runs the blood of a forgotten empire.

My love for writing poetry allowed me to describe what I had seen and the people I met. As the weeks became months, then years, I started to collect anecdotes and stories from my customers. The stories that follow are some of them. They are from meetings with explorers that had been to the heart of the Amazon to people that knew Rudyard Kipling.

I found that the world on my doorstep was as exciting as any far pavilion. As life went by I came to realise the splendour of this amazing planet is at our fingertips, all we have to do is capture it.

In the pages that follow you may get some idea of the affection that I have for my unique spot on our planet.

I do hope you enjoy the stories as much as I have enjoyed writing them. They all have a common thread running through them. My daily life as a mobile repairman and the humble sewing machine. Many of the stories are unconnected. That is why the series title of *Random Threads* is such a good description. Sit back, put the kettle on, and enjoy.

SIMPLANTEX
– Simple Planning of Textiles

My modelling for the family firm Simplantex started young. Here I am aged two, posing for my mother's finest invention, the Rain Cape. It sold in the 100,000's all over the world from Iceland to New Zealand.

Here I am for another brochure aged 5. This was my first trip to London to the studio. I had never seen so many people and houses in my life. I thought I had found the centre of the world.

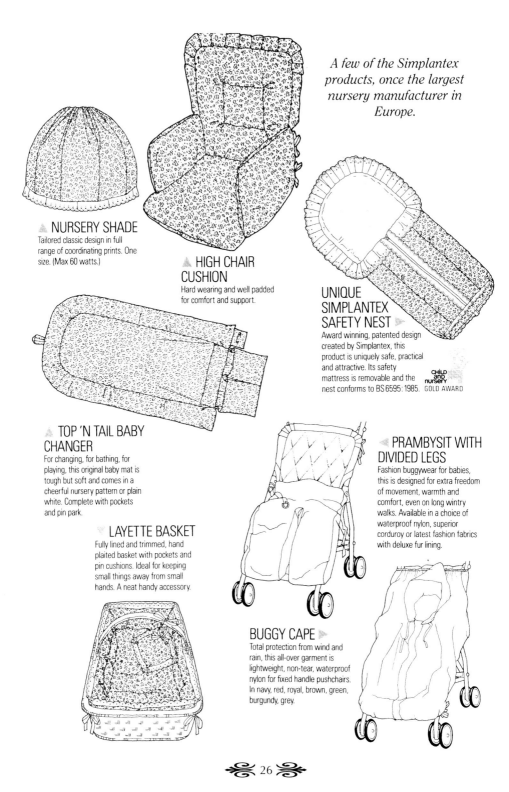

A few of the Simplantex products, once the largest nursery manufacturer in Europe.

NURSERY SHADE
Tailored classic design in full range of coordinating prints. One size. (Max 60 watts.)

HIGH CHAIR CUSHION
Hard wearing and well padded for comfort and support.

UNIQUE SIMPLANTEX SAFETY NEST
Award winning, patented design created by Simplantex, this product is uniquely safe, practical and attractive. Its safety mattress is removable and the nest conforms to BS 6595: 1985.

CHILD and nursery GOLD AWARD

TOP 'N TAIL BABY CHANGER
For changing, for bathing, for playing, this original baby mat is tough but soft and comes in a cheerful nursery pattern or plain white. Complete with pockets and pin park.

LAYETTE BASKET
Fully lined and trimmed, hand plaited basket with pockets and pin cushions. Ideal for keeping small things away from small hands. A neat handy accessory.

PRAMBYSIT WITH DIVIDED LEGS
Fashion buggywear for babies, this is designed for extra freedom of movement, warmth and comfort, even on long wintry walks. Available in a choice of waterproof nylon, superior corduroy or latest fashion fabrics with deluxe fur lining.

BUGGY CAPE
Total protection from wind and rain, this all-over garment is lightweight, non-tear, waterproof nylon for fixed handle pushchairs. In navy, red, royal, brown, green, burgundy, grey.

My beautiful Daimler, saved from the auction rooms by my wife.

Wish Hill in Willingdon with the old post office behind. This is a timeless photo and except for a few things like the cars and burglar alarm it could have been taken 50 years ago. The village post office by the telephone box is 400 years old.

A typical East Sussex Country Lane

Eastourne and its only skyscraper where Roger Moore once lived in the Penthouse.

ATTACK

As a travelling repairman I started to get calls to all sorts of places from schools, factories, hospitals and homes.

I visited the most unexpected places to fix sewing machines. For example I went to Children's Treasures in George Street, Hastings. They sell dolls and other toys. You wouldn't think that they needed a sewing machine but they do. They have a doll's hospital for the repair of sick dolls from all over the country. In the hospital they have a pillar machine for sewing plastic arms onto the dolls. It is a very special industrial machine indeed.

Glyndebourne Opera House, a few miles in the opposite direction, always had a hand-sewing machine behind the stage for emergency costume repairs during the performance. It had to be a hand machine so that it would not make any noise during the performances. I now have their superb fiddle base machine in my collection.

These machines all needed my special attention. Each morning I would set off with a list of addresses and a packed lunch. I would travel from one business or home to another, working my art on the poor machines bringing them back to life and ready for work again.

I had just started to get established when I had a call from a lady asking me to call in the evening as it was not suitable for me to call during the day. Because I desperately needed the money I reluctantly agreed. She gave me her address, a house called Salem in the middle of nowhere.

Now I had just seen *Salem's Lot* on TV with that chap out of Starskey and Hutch. It was all about evil goings on around the town of Salem in New England.

Everything about the call had seemed funny and I became a bit apprehensive about it. I told my wife that if I was not back by 10 o'clock to call out the cavalry. She laughed but I was not so sure.

I was on tenterhooks because the week before I had had a call from a commune, way out in the sticks. They were some kind of religious revivalists. They had their own school, hospital and church and they made all their own clothes. All the women wore scarves over their heads and aprons. They looked like an English version of the Amish.

They were all very pleasant and soon I was busily working away in the main hall of the commune fixing the sewing machines. Then a bell rang out.

Suddenly everyone dropped to their knees. I was left looking slightly bemused as they mumbled words between their clenched hands. I was not even sure to whom they were praying. I sat quietly for a few minutes until they finished and then we all carried on as if nothing had happened.

They were so isolated that they had almost no idea about what was going on in the outside world and they asked me many questions. I was left thinking that, instead of paying their bill, a bag would be put over my head and I would never be seen again as I would be slaving away in the Australian outback somewhere sewing aprons and praying to a giant rock.

In fact they paid cash and blessed me for my fine efforts.

Anyway, back to the story. Still being a bit wary, on the night that I had my evening visit I found the address. A crooked wooden plaque nailed to a post read SALEM. It was a large old house up a dark drive. The headlights lit up the ramshackle garden that had brambles hanging over clawing at my car as I drove slowly up the drive.

The house looked menacing in the dark. A single light swung in the breeze over the doorway throwing shadows across the front porch. I was not happy about the whole situation at all and I was afraid that things were going to get worse. Mobile phones were rare and I could not afford one anyway so there was no escape! Once inside there was no turning back. I braced myself and rang the doorbell.

A huge woman came to the door. She appeared larger because the door was above the entrance by a few steps but, even so, in the dim light of the swinging lamp she was taller than I, and a menacing sight.

She calmly ushered me into the living room. There sat a Singer 507, alone, on a large oak table. I immediately noticed that to work on the machine I would have to have my back to both doors that led into the room. I was not at all happy. However I came up with a cunning plan. By moving the table slightly, with the excuse of getting closer to the power point, I dragged it in front of the curtains.

No sooner had the lady left the room than I opened the curtains. Because it was pitch dark outside, the window acted as a mirror giving me a perfect reflected view of the room behind. Feeling slightly more secure I started to work on the machine as quickly as possible. Unfortunately a plastic feed-drive-gear had sheared underneath the machine and the job was dragging on. It didn't help that I kept glancing up at the window to check behind me as I worked.

Everything had gone well. I was still uneasy because the wind outside was making the branches tap against the dark windows and the door behind me kept creaking.

The new gear slipped into place and I was busy timing up the lower shaft when I heard a noise behind me. I looked up at the window to see the reflection of the woman coming into the room. In her hand, as clear as day, was a knife.

In one instant movement I leapt up, knocking over my toolbox, and twisted around to face my assailant. She screamed, startled by my instinctive reaction for self-preservation. Out of her other hand, not the one holding the knife, fell a potato.

Yes, she was peeling a spud for her supper and had come to see if I would like a cup of tea. I felt such an idiot. I calmed her down and put all my tools back in the box and we both had a good laugh over a cup of tea.

I look after that Singer to this day. When I visit we still smile about that dark winter's night when, in my paranoia, I mistook a kind old lady preparing supper as a murderous assailant.

MARCH

Ti's time to stop and stare,
To breathe the fresh spring air,
Because March has finally come,
And the battle over winter won,
Now daffodils dance and laugh,
Along both sides of our little path,
We look forward to the sun,
And lazy days having fun,
But all to soon the cold will return,
And for this breath of spring we shall yearn.

ALEX. I. ASKAROFF

COUNTRY WAYS – SPRING

I set off at the crack of dawn on my usual rounds. It was a surprisingly warm day for the time of year. There was no wind and the cold frosts of previous weeks had been replaced with a misty damp. I drove along the A27, turning off the main Brighton road at the tiny hamlet of Wilmington.

Once off the main drag I was suddenly alone. The only place the road leads to is old houses and farm tracks. The Giants Rest, the local pub, looked quiet. No one was stirring at this time of day except the local tabby cat pawing one of the windows, idly chasing a fly. It looked like it had had a night on the tiles.

A little further up the narrow road which was made for little more than the occasional horse and cart, now tarmaced for our modern vehicles, stands the remains of Wilmington Priory. The brick open-drain that runs down the side of the quaint postcard cottages was, at one time, where the occupants would throw out their daily waste to run down to the stream.

Just a few of the priory walls still stand, defiant against time and nature. Although it was Henry V that was responsible for the priory's downfall most were torn down by our famous Henry VIII. In one of his tantrums at the all-powerful Roman Catholic Church he really got the hump. It was after the refusal by the Pope to allow Henry the first of his famous divorces that he went on his destroying rampage politely known as *The dissolution of the monasteries.*

Then, becoming smarter, he promptly stopped destroying these wonderful places and started selling them off to his noblemen for a fair sum. They say that it was Henry's men that ransacked Thomas Becket's shrine in Canterbury and came away with over 7 tons of gold, silver and jewels in their plunder.

The Priory lies at the feet of a giant, the Long Man. His outline is carved into the chalk hillside. He is some 230 feet (75 metres) high and dominates the landscape for miles around. Exactly who carved him is still a mystery. His history is lost forever in the mists of time as he stands dominant between two huge posts. Some say that he was for pagan rituals, but nobody really knows. Eternally he surveys the lands below him as we mortals rush past, like ants, in our insignificant flurry of existence.

Once beyond the Priory and Long Man the farmland rolls out before the road for miles. The fabulous South Downs spread for a hundred miles towards the West Country and the Cornish coast. There is an old saying –

If the Downs be wearing her cap,
Be sure you're in fer a drap.

Translated to *it is going to rain, and hard.*

The old gatekeeper back at the family firm would come out to greet me each morning as I arrived at the factory.

"Good morning Mr Hollibone. What's the weather going to do today?" I would ask.

He would glance around the factory wall towards the Downs in the distance and give me his opinion. He was never wrong. Today the low cloud was hanging around in patches like a cloth cap on the Downs. Rain was on the way and old Hollibone would be telling me to keep a rain coat handy.

On a little further I came to Lullington Church, known as the smallest church in England. It was once much larger but a fire destroyed the main building leaving just the entrance. The vicar, determined not to lose his parish, converted the remains into the tiny church we see today. It has 20 seats and some standing room.

The church is up a small path and nestled into the downland. There are regular services. Gravestones in a small copse of woods speckled with snowdrops in springtime mark the few graves that survive. Some of the stones stand at precarious angles defying balance. They all demand to be read, declaring that we never forget the people that shaped this countryside.

Further down the road we come to a larger church, a few farm buildings and set in the distant hillside, another chalk monument to the past. A huge white horse overlooks a fantastic viewpoint known as The High & Over. Its commanding views over the Cuckmere valley have been appointed by

British Nature as a point of *outstanding natural beauty.*

You can see for miles over the Cuckmere vale. The river meanders lazily through the middle of it out to the sea. The low sun was catching the water and throwing a thousand glittering diamonds into the sky. A small row of coastguard cottages stand vigilant against smugglers that no longer creep upriver at dead of night with their booty of tea and spirits. Not forgetting, of course, some brandy for the parson.

It was here that Morgan Freeman and Kevin Costner landed, in the movie *Robin Hood: Prince of Thieves* with the backdrop of these cliffs. Also for part of the British dog fight in the film *Pearl Harbour.* They are known locally as the Seven Sisters and their sheer white-chalk faces are capped with bonnets of downland grass. Each day they catch the first glimpses of morning light as the sun creeps over the horizon from our French neighbours.

On the other side of the downs, out of sight is the River Ouse. This is where Virginia Woolf walked out of her Rodmell home one night, filled her dressing gown pockets with stones and stepped into the cold river to end her pain. No more could the sparrows talk to her in Greek or the cries of lost souls torment her.

My first call of the morning was Charleston Manor and as I turned into the long gravel drive, two perfect rows of yew trees greeted me. They stood neatly to attention like guards at the Palace as I drove past.

Pheasant clucked about on the lawn foraging for their breakfast among the decaying debris of winter. The main drive came to a halt in a large circle at the main doors to the manor.

I spent the next hour servicing a Riccar 990 in the garden cottage where the groundsman used to live when Lord and Lady Burleigh ruled the roost. People that live away now own the main house. They visit during the warmer summer months and disappear with the swallows when autumn nears. The Burleigh's summer fetes and tea mornings are now just fond memories for the old folk to reminisce about.

My next call was off to the Sisters of Mercy in Seaford. One of their sisters had returned from Madagascar and, having a passion for sewing, had promptly broken all three of the sewing machines at her convent and then the one next door just for good measure! Over the years I have supplied hand machines for their mission in Madagascar where they train people to operate them. The humble sewing machine can mean the difference between a life of poverty and a comfortable living to a local family.

After a short time all the machines were running well and I hit the road for the next customer. A Singer 760 *Touch 'n' Sew* (renamed *Touch 'n' Throw* due to its problems) with reverse trouble proved tricky but it came up well in the end.

I travelled North in search of my next call at Olive's Farm where I was greeted by a collie dog with more mud on him than I have ever seen on a dog. He seemed pleased to see me but I was not so keen to play. I managed to ring the doorbell covered in muddy paw prints down the front of my jacket. The owner looked at me and just wiped me down as if I was one of her children.

I started on her machine as she made me a wonderful cup of Moroccan coffee. It is half-strong dark coffee with half-boiled milk, hot and sweet. She had visited Morocco 17 times and loved the way the Arabs pinched her bum all the time. Apparently they love large blondes and cannot help themselves. On her last visit a beaming guide grabbed her from behind. He told her she had made his day and he was going straight home to make love to his wife and dream of having a blonde baby.

After servicing her Bernina Minimatic I made my way back along the road past huge elms that stood bare in the midday light. It was still, not a breath of wind to move their branches into life. Around their huge bases were clumps of crocus, piercing through the grass in all the colours of the rainbow, bravely flowering in the cold. All foretelling the spring to come. I wondered how many of the elms might end up in the coffin-maker's workshop as it is still a favourite timber for the discerning classes for their final resting place.

I came out onto the road facing a property with a boar carved above the front door and the builder's date of 1558 below it. Visions of these wild beasts roasting on an open fire came to mind. Boar was popular meat amongst the forest folk for many centuries in this wooded part of Sussex.

History is everywhere you look if you want to see it. The year 1558 was the year that the daughter of Anne Boleyn came to the throne and one of our most famous monarchs, Elizabeth I ruled Britain.

One more stop in Uckfield that has the *Yucky Ucky* (the River Uck) flowing through it. The river is so nicknamed as it has never, to anyone's knowledge, run clear. It is always a sludge-brown colour.

The machine I came to see was a neglected 221k made in 1954 and bought from a junk shop on a whim. It had cost her thirty pounds. It is always someone else who finds these gems isn't it?

I waxed lyrical about the wonderful machine while the new owner looked on in quiet bewilderment. As she sat down to use it for the very first time all became clear. She had been an avid quilter and Bernina fan but, in a second was converted and fell in love with a battered 50-year-old featherweight now christened *Lucky*.

The East Sussex part of the South Downs are the most gentle and so the most appealing. The soft undulations of green hold a beauty that has to be seen.

TICKLED WITH A FEATHER

England is set out much like a large quilt. Before the coming of motorways the country had remained little-changed for centuries.

Towns and villages needed to be no more than a day's walk from each other. The reason for that was simple. If you were taking cattle, sheep or pigs to market you needed to get them there in the morning, sell them and get back home again. The farthest you could live from your village was just less than half a day's walk.

The whole of England evolved in this way. A trip to market would be a day's walk there and back. If you looked at a map of the country you would see each town and village connected by a system of roads and tracks all about 7 to 15 miles apart. A thousand little spiders' webs all interconnecting.

This system remained unchanged until canals, railways and motorways cut through the land changing the shape of our country that had been the same since Roman times.

Steve, a fisherman in Fairlight, lives in one such village. Dropped onto the east side of the hill from Hastings, the picturesque village has sweeping views across the coast to Rye and our blot on the landscape, Dungeness Power Station.

Hastings is where William I built his first castle after landing on English soil. There is an old joke. They had to make William king as all the rest of the invaders were called Norman. Get it? I know it's weak but never fear they get worse!

Steve had been waiting since before Christmas for his big Singer 212g industrial machine. I set it up for him for his boat tarpaulins. He had been patiently waiting for me to find him a twin-needle machine. I tracked one down at Graham Cresswells in Sherwood, Nottingham.

With us living on the southern-most point of the country it was quite a trek up north to the Midlands to pick up the machine. We were not mugged by Robin Hood and arrived safely after a few detours to visit family near Birmingham and friends in Norfolk.

When we delivered the machine Yana and I dropped the Singer off at the crack of dawn and asked Steve if he knew of a good café for breakfast. Being a fisherman Steve knew the difference between a normal breakfast and a real man's one. He recommended the café that the lads all used down on Hastings seafront. The cafe is an old hut that was used to dry out the fishing nets and had been converted to a small café. The drying-huts are a unique site on the beach. The tall, dark, narrow, wooden buildings stand proud against the Hastings skyline.

As we arrived on the beach the sign above the door said *Closed.*

I asked at the fish shop below and was told to just go in. Mavis only puts that sign on the door to keep people away. Well, I thought, she could use a week at some sales seminars, that's for sure!

Anyway she knocked us up a wonderful fry-up as we sat overlooking the coast. It was a rough, overcast, slate-grey day with a strong southwesterly coming off the sea. The wind had churned up the Channel and the tips of the waves were white and wild. Seagulls were diving in and out of the troughs and teasing the fishermen with their cries.

The sea had thrown debris up the beach and frothy-spume tumbled over the pebbles like froth blown from a washing bowl.

The talk in the café, amongst the stranded fishermen, was of the nets that had been left out at sea that no one could get to in this rough weather. They were all blaming the BBC as the weather forecast had been for a northerly wind and a calming sea. Typically wrong again!

The other sad talk was of the seven brave young fishermen that had just perished with their boat in the Irish Sea. Although the life rafts had been found no soul had survived. A poignant reminder of the danger and hardships that the men face daily to earn a living. It is a fact that they have one of the most dangerous jobs in Britain with higher fatalities than firemen and policemen.

After a good feed and a chat we headed towards home with a bag of fresh cod for supper. On the way we had one more stop, at Annie Bonner's.

Annie told me of her days in the sewing room when she was relocated during the war. At the end of each week, on Friday afternoon, the whole sewing room would stop to clean and oil the machines. Oiling the machine is always a point of discussion. Just how much should you oil a sewing machine?

Well this is what she told me. After cleaning the machine they would take a feather, dip it in the machine oil, shake it a little and then proceed to tickle the machine all over. This had the effect of putting a tiny but effective bit of oil around the moving parts of the sewing machine. If, during the week, the line manager would hear a noisy machine she would say, "That needs a tickle with a feather."

During all the years that Annie worked at the factory they never had a machine break down with bearing failure. Now you know what to do if your old industrial machine starts to complain. Simply give it a tickle with a feather.

The Holy Trinity in Highhurstwood is one of the most unsual churches in my area. East Sussex has the highest concentration of ancient churches anywhere in the world.

A PERFECT DAY

Spring had been a long time coming. The long cold months of winter had smothered any spring-like enthusiasm that I had had but it had arrived today! A clear blue sky and a warm breeze heralded the new season in full force.

It was as if my eyes were suddenly open. The whole countryside was alive with willows sprouting and catkins budding from branches screaming *let me out!* A profusion of spring plants lined the roadsides and fields. Every flower, from daffodils to primroses, had popped their heads up as if in recognition that winter had fled. Today England really was a green and pleasant land.

My morning started with a quick trip up to Buxted to an old Singer pulled reluctantly out of the dusty loft for a pair of curtains. As I arrived the village school bus was being loaded with children on their way to another day at the village primary.

The machine gave me a good fight but before long it was dragged out of retirement and sewing beautifully. I was not too sure how pleased the owner was – now having to make the curtains. I had a sneaky feeling she would have much preferred her husband to fork out for a new set at the local soft-furnishings shop in the High Street. Still, no sooner done than I was off to my next call towards the Sussex-Kent border.

This was an unusual repair. A Toyota industrial with a timing problem that turned out to be the tip of a needle jammed in the hook. It put up a fair struggle but, in the end, succumbed to my enthusiastic attack and superior endurance.

Before long I was off again along a small country lane near Burwash, to my next call. Burwash is famous for, among other things, our poet and novelist Rudyard Kipling, of *Jungle Book* fame. He spent the latter years of his life at Bateman's, a lovely manor built in 1634 for a local ironmaster.

Not a lot of people know that our part of England cradled one of the first major iron industrial areas in the world.

Kipling lived at the manor for over 30 years and whilst there he wrote such stories as *Puck of Pook's Hill* and *Rewards and Fairies*. His ghost still lives there now. When you visit Bateman's you can feel his presence all around.

Years ago I met an old lady, Alice, whose parents were in service to the Kiplings and, as a child, she knew Rudyard very well because he often played with her. She called me out to service her machine. Alice was now living in a warden-assisted home off the Burwash High Street. She was amazing. She had hardly ever been out of the village.

Now that may seem extraordinary to us today but life for Alice was very different. Her knowledge about things outside Burwash was almost non-existent but in the village she knew everyone and everything – and I mean everything! She told me where the well was, pointing out a drain-cover just off the High Street. She told me who had fallen down the well in 1924 and how he had been rescued. She told me who went off to war and never came back. She told me who the blacksmith was and what he got up to. Her mind was electric!

As I fixed her machine we travelled back in time together. Back to a Burwash of the past. She had a beautiful, soft Sussex accent that only survives among rural folk born and bred. It was almost musical as she spoke. What a delight it was to listen to her reminiscing.

Then she mentioned Rudyard Kipling.

"What?" I said, "You remember Rudyard Kipling?"

"Oh yes! I remember him as if it were yesterday. He used to play with me out the back of the kitchen."

I was so intrigued. "At Bateman's?" I asked.

"Of course! Mind you I was no more than a child but, as I remember it, he made me a cart of sorts out of a treadle sewing-machine lid and some wheels. He would push me around for hours as my mother cooked in the kitchen."

"My father worked as a gardener so the Kiplings employed them both. Mind you, it was her that wore the pants in that house!"

"What do you mean?" I replied hating to break her flow.

"She wore the pants all right, the mistus (lady of the house). It was a big mistake to cross her. Even Mr Kipling took to hiding sometimes."

"Go on! You're kidding me."

"Oh no! I have seen him, more than once, go and hide in the outside lavvy, down the garden. He would be in there for ages. Mrs Kipling would give up hunting for him after a while. Then out he would creep with handfuls of paper, toilet paper, full of scribbling."

"You mean he wrote some of his stories in the outside toilet? Hiding from his wife!" I said in astonishment.

"I think that's about the long and short of it," she smiled. "She made my dad cut holes in the Yew hedges so that she could peek at the prisoners working in the gardens. Just in case they were being lapsy (lazy)."

"Get away! You're pulling my leg," I laughed.

"No! God's truth. When they had German prisoners to do the gardening she would creep about spying on them. Making sure they weren't up to no good. When the yew flowered, we called the red fruit berries that held the green seeds 'snotty-gogs' as they were all slimy. Now that's an old Sussex word for you."

"I remember old Mr Kipling always forgot to order the right groceries. He used to cuss the stupid boy at the shop in Heathfield High Street and then he'd say's he might as well go and pick them up himself. We used to ride in a big old Rolls Royce and pick up the veg. When we got to the shop it weren't the boy that forgot at all. It was himself escaping for a few hours. I'm not saying he did not love her dearly but she was a hard woman. Hard but fair. Oh she was the mistus all right!"

I left Alice with images of Rudyard writing some of his great poems on loo paper while hiding in the outside lavvy. What a wonder Alice was! As for Rudyard Kipling, you could say that he wrote at his convenience!

I only meet people like her once in a blue moon. Amazingly, a few years later, I met the grocery boy whose job it was to deliver the fruit and vegetables to the Kiplings. He remembered Alice and the scoldings from

Mrs Kipling for forgetting some of the vegetables.

My next call was to a farm set in the High Weald, a stretch of heaven that runs in a ridge from East Sussex to Kent. I was calling on a hop farm. As I arrived Mrs Hillbury and her husband were busy getting things ready for the new season.

Hops are an essential ingredient in all good beers and lagers and, as most people know, British beer is the best although some of it is so strong it will put hair on your chest and make you think the world is ending.

Unfortunately some sneaky scientists a few years ago figured out how to remove the essence from the hops. This means that hops do not have to be stored any more. Hop essence from years ago can be dropped into the brew to give it that special preservative and bitter taste so needed for quality beer.

Many of these farms are still run as they have been for centuries. Hop vines are grown over sheets of coconut matting up long chestnut poles that were harvested from the local forests where they have been coppiced in the same way since Norman times.

In times past, during the hop-picking season, whole families would arrive from London and spend a few weeks' holiday picking the flowers. Families stayed in shantytown style tin-huts along the edges of the fields. During the hot autumn days the women, with pinnies and scarves around their heads, would pick all day while their children played around the fields, running wild in the countryside away from the city smog.

The huts sometimes had little more than a bedsheet pinned up to separate families. For a short time there was a spirit of the old days that came back to life. Then, as suddenly as they arrived, they all went back on the buses and headed for the smoke (London). The fields that had echoed with cockney laughter lay silent once more and young children were home to dream of harvest time in hop country.

One of my friends was a *hop-child* and I lived these memories through his eyes as he talked of those days with a tear close-by.

There were also downsides for the farmers. Hops have a natural sedative effect like a sleeping drug and it is hell getting everyone up in the mornings as they sleep the sleep of the dead. Mrs Hillbury used her tractor to wake them all. She would run up and down the sheds revving the old Perkins diesel engine until everyone was awake.

While parking, Colin the beekeeper passed me, going off to smoke out his bees and check his hives for the first time this year. Smoking calms the bees before opening their hive. The bees are all getting out of bed after a long break and getting back to work on the spring flowers.

"Off to get your first sting?" I shouted.

He just laughed and waved. If he does not sort out his hives at the right time the queen takes off and looks for a new home followed by her faithful swarm. I knew I would taste his honey in a few months. My wife's family have kept bees on their farm in Hereford for decades and it tastes like no other honey.

After dropping off Mrs Hillbury's Bernina at her farm – I had replaced the cam gear, a common problem with Berninas – I wriggled my way down country lanes to Punnetts Town.

This area of the Weald is Mad Jack Fuller country. Mad Jack, whose actual name was John, came from a wealthy iron-working family that boasted, back in the 1700s, that only they could make great cannon. The discovery of huge iron and coal deposits on the land here brought them untold wealth. Then the manufacture of cannon brought more wealth and distinction.

Fuller Cannon lined the coasts of England to protect her shores. They were dragged into battle at Waterloo and brought Napoleon to his knees. They thundered around the world as Britain became master of two-thirds of it. They were hauled up the Khyber Pass in India and across the plains of Africa. Fuller Cannon had become part of the British Empire and the Fuller name moved to its place in history. Local gossip tells that Fuller cannons lined the decks of the HMS Victory as Nelson sailed victorious into history and immortality in the Battle of Trafalgar.

Out of all the follies that Jack built around this area, the Brightling Needle, stands out the most. Built on an ancient beacon site it stands 640 feet (about 210 metres) above sea level on the brow of a hill. They say that *as long as it stands no one will forget him.*

Locally he is more fondly remembered as *Honest Jack* because he refused a peerage apparently saying, "I was born Jack Fuller and so I shall die."

However Jack Fuller was a boastful man and, one day, in a bet with his fellow MPs he said that the views were so magnificent from his Sussex Manor that he could see no less than five church steeples. When he got back from the House (Houses of Parliament) he realised he could only see four. Never one to be outwitted he quickly got some local builders to knock up an extra church steeple on the edge of his land.

When his visitors arrived they counted all 5 church steeples. He won the wager and the steeple is still there today. He has an odd-shaped triangular grave in the local churchyard. Legend has it that he sits there, at a table, with his cat and a bottle of red wine.

My next call was down a tiny lane where I had to park and walk the rest of the way on foot along a narrow path that we call a twitten. The path leads only to Mrs Jenny at Blackbird Cottage. The path winds its way lazily down to her place and is hardly wider than my shoulders. The ground was layered with clinker from her fire. She sprinkles the ashes over the path to keep it from getting waterlogged in winter.

Halfway down I stopped to soak up the countryside.

You can see why pagan rituals were performed to herald in spring at this time of year. Everything has come to life. After months of cold inactivity the very earth itself was breathing.

Bright yellow celandine flowers were popping up in the meadows like water lilies on a green-velvet lake. Wild periwinkle was everywhere creeping out of the hedgerows looking like bits of the blue sky dropped to the ground.

There was almost no sound, just a quiet hush over the countryside. In the distance a horse whinnied and a cow replied. A dog barked on the farm down in the valley but otherwise all was quiet. They say that, on special days like these, sound travels for miles and a dog barking in a Sussex pub can be heard by and replied to by one in Kent.

After dilly-dallying for too long I fixed yet another Bernina. They go wrong just as much as any other machine. This time the bearing had slipped out of alignment causing the machine to miss stitches. Mrs Jenny's old Alsatian followed me up the path before deciding enough was enough and slumping in a sunny spot for the rest of the morning. She looked at me as I went as if to say *if you were smart you would stay too.*

There are many pubs, around the country, that I pass on my travels. They have a thousand names. Everything from the Rat & Parrot to The White Hart. Many are named after local heroes such as Jack Cade and the like. The one that always makes me wonder is the *Kings Head*. I pass pubs with this name all over England.

Some may be a reference to Charles the First who had his head chopped off – one way to get instant relief from a headache I suppose!

It was a chilly morning back in January 1649 that King Charles stepped up to the scaffold with the drums rolling. He had had his tailor make two shirts, one over the other, so that the crowd would not see him shiver and mistake it for fear. He had complete faith in God and a belief that he had a divine right to rule England. Rather than renounce his rights he would face his maker.

Oliver Cromwell had forced his hand and, with his life, the King would pay the ultimate price. As he reached the executioner he pushed a gold sovereign into the hooded axeman's hand – for the axe man to give a clean blow – then he knelt and folded his black hair forward over the block.

The axeman's blade fell with a sickening thud. A huge sigh rose from the onlookers. Few people had really believed that the execution would take place. The axeman held the dripping head of the King up to the crowd but no one cheered. His last words were still in their ears, "I go from a corruptible to an incorruptible Crown, where no disturbance can be."

For the next decade Cromwell ruled our land and brought about many changes, some good, some bad. For example St. Paul's in London fell into a terrible state of disrepair. At one point, the church was so bad that a road was knocked through with shops and seamstresses and the chancel was used to stable horses. Hard to believe now.

My next stop is at Heathfield to sharpen some scissors and give a bit of technical advice on making blinds for a conservatory. I apologised for the smell of the fireplace that had stuck to my shoes after the walk down the clinker path earlier. I dropped off a model 221 Featherweight manual for the customer, stopped for a coffee and finally headed back across my beautiful corner of England towards the sea glimmering on the horizon with the Downs lying like a sleeping giant across the skyline.

I was full of the joys of Spring like a new-born lamb. For today, after long weeks of drab and dull weather it really was a perfect spring day.

Typical tourists! Chartwell, the home of Winston Churchill just over the border in Kent. Walking around his home it feels as if he has just popped out for a spot of lunch.

Once little more than gravel pits where I poached perch and eel. The Old Crumbles now Sovereign Harbour. It was the old artillery range where we used to sneak in to find shells, now one of the premier harbours in Europe.

The plaque below the Jack Cade memorial near Heathfield. Jack Cade was amongst the rebel leaders who marched on London many years ago and met a grizzly end. Today he would probably be the head of a union.

This is the gun emplacement at Pevensey Castle. The castle has stood for 2000 years. First built as a roman shore fort, then rebuilt by the Normans. Later reinforced during other wars and finally in WWII. The clever camoflage made the gun emplacement difficult to spot in the event of a German invasion.

DIFFERENT DAYS

The morning ahead was going to be a busy one. It even included one customer who had suffered a stroke and forgotten how to use her Singer 185k sewing machine.

I dropped Yana off to work at Marks & Spencer by 6.30am and headed along Eastbourne seafront toward Beachy Head.

At the Carpet Gardens workers were already busy pulling some of the early flowering plants and trimming up the immaculately kept gardens that Eastbourne is world famous for. Although it was a busy day I could not really drag someone out of bed at 6.30 so I had an hour to waste before I had to knock on my customer's door in Newhaven, some 11 miles across the downs.

I poodled up along King Edward's Parade soaking in the glorious early morning. The sea was a myriad of diamonds thrown over a blue duvet. Gulls called to each other circling high on the early thermals that lifted off the cliff edges, the cliff edges where wild wallflowers gripped precariously on the chalk faces.

An early heat wave and a southerly wind had brought the red sand of the Sahara over to Sussex and laid it gently and almost invisibly on everything. With the sea breeze came the heady scent of wild and exotic places from far away.

This spring had been perfect, the sort of spring that you only remember as a child in the endless summer days of youth. The daffodils had danced in the breeze and the banks of the narrow Sussex roads were strewn with primrose and celandine. The whole countryside was in celebration of a new season.

As I drove higher up toward Beachy Head the magnificent South Downs opened up before me, miles of open rolling downland with sheep and cattle grazing in the green pastures. The hedgerows were alive with sparrows squabbling for nesting spaces and in the fields skylark were busy picking out prime sites in the low scrub.

The skylark is not a beautiful bird it looks a little like a large sparrow but when it sings the world stops. The skylark steals the show with a bright clear warbling song that reaches down into your soul and pulls your heartstrings. They must be attached to your face muscles because when you hear a skylark sing you cannot help but smile.

I parked the Land Rover and soaked in the early morning on the South Downs and breathed in the heady aroma that I am sure only exists in this one place on earth. There were a few people walking dogs, a farmer moving bales of feed-hay in his tractor and endless miles of sky, sea and downland.

Cowslips sprinkled the green of the downs with buttery yellow drops on pale green stems and in the hedgerow wild cherry blossomed protected by its tough neighbour, the hawthorn, who's delicate flower is held behind spikes as fierce as a hedgehogs bristles.

Before I knew, half an hour had disappeared and I made my way along the winding road past the hamlet of Birling Gap and on to the main coast road at East Dean. By 7.30 I was standing at my customers door knocking with eager enthusiasm at the start of a new day.

Through out the morning each call had gone as planned and by midday I was making my way up to one of my favourite customers in Sidley called Ron Saunders. I had called on Ron and his wife many times and Ron always engaged me with his lovely Sussex accent.

"Morning Alec! Gonna be a nice one agin'." Ron said more as a statement than a greeting.

"Yep! It has turned out nice it's sure to be a blaster this afternoon if the sun stays out." I added

"Wife's buggerin' machine has gone wrong agin'." Ron said standing over the Italian Necchi machine with a look of disgust.

"Tess looks a bit thin." I said looking down at his old golden Labrador.

"Vet's put it on pills poor dog, says it's too fat. I'm takin' it off today. Prefer it to be fat 'n' happy."

I had to admit on my last call the dog was doing a good impersonation of a seal on legs. The diet may do the beast good.

"I could do with losing a bit myself." I said patting my stomach.

"Couldn't we all Alec, couldn't we all. Here's the wife now, she'll tell yer' what's wrong with the damn thing."

With that, Ron disappeared into his back garden pulling on his tatty tweed jacket and old cap then trotting off down the path to his little patch of heaven. I never saw Ron without his jacket even in the middle of summer.

Ron was from an old Sussex family and could tell tales from long ago. His father was a woodsman who supplied locally coppiced chestnut to the famous Herstmonceux Trug Company, for their trugs and seasoned willow for cricket bats. The tradition of coppicing had gone on over the great forests of the Sussex Weald with little change since Roman times.

Before too long I had the old Necchi purring along and was ready to hit the road for a well-needed break and a spot of lunch. Ron came back as I finished.

"Bag of manure and a tenner do you boy?" Ron chirped.

"Do me fine Ron, that will do me fine."

I never charged Ron the full amount. He had become more of a friend over the years than a paying customer. On the way along the garden path we chatted about his garden and what flowers he was bringing on for the summer.

With the manure loaded and money in my pocket I started the trusty Land Rover waved goodbye to Ron who was leaning over his gate. I pointed the car homeward for a well-deserved break.

Not the best deal of the day but certainly the most enjoyable, I thought as I drove. Mind you, the Ron's of this world were few and far between and each meeting with the old Sussex man with his soft lyrical accent was a pleasure.

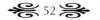

THE SUSSEX TONGUE

The Sussex tongue is soft and sweet,

Laced with skylark in summer wheat.

It ripples like a babbling brook,

Thick and rich with a Cornish hook.

The Sussex tongue is almost gone,

To be lost amongst the meadow song.

In years to come you may search in vain,

For the Sussex tongue won't rise again.

Alex. I. Askaroff

The Beachy Head pub with one of the most beautiful landscapes on earth behind.

A twitten in East Dean. The word twitten is a Sussex word for a narrow path. this is a particularly pretty one leading to the village green.

BUXTED BONANZA

I knew it was going to be one of those days when the second of my morning's customers was as bad as the first! She was moaning about everything. The weather, the state of the country, her grass growing too fast – I was happy to escape, hoping that my next customer could at least have a smile on her face.

The day before had been completely different. One 90-year-old that had watched, from his garden swing, bi-planes shoot down Zeppelins during the first World War. Then there was the old, salty seadog that had taken part in the attack on the Bismarck along with the HMS Hood. There was the lovely old man that had been in the first wave of the D-Day landings on Normandy. His job was to set up the radar station on the beach. Then off to a wonderful lady who told me of her visit to her old friend in Siam who just happened to be a princess. Each call seemed to hold a wealth of stories – unlike today.

I was just being optimistic, hoping for far too much because the call was no better. As my customer opened the door she had a scowl on her face like a kicked cat. Still, in my usual professional manner I got down to fixing her machine and before long, I managed to extract myself from her grasp and hit the road.

My last customer of the morning was a sweet old dear. The Knights had retired down to East Sussex and had a little house in a village, called Buxted, some 20 miles north of my home town of Eastbourne. Buxted is on the verge of the great Ashdown Forest where King Henry VIII hunted wild boar and chased one of his maids-in-waiting Anne Boleyn, later to become one of his wives with a rather nasty ending.

The weather was overcast and cold. A typical early British summer and the main reason for England being such a green and pleasant land. All that water has the one beneficial effect of keeping everything a lush green.

Mrs Knight had called me out to fix her Singer 527 that had suddenly stopped. I knew it was probably the gears but did not want to tell her over the phone until I was sure. By the time I walked up the pretty garden path lined with pinks and a few remaining bluebells I was in a bad mood. It is amazing how it can rub off – other people's moods that is. All the moaning and groaning during the morning had taken its toll. Mrs Knight was the last call of the morning, a morning that had seemed to drag like a boring school class from when I was a kid.

Mrs Knight's husband had died some time ago and, as I walked in, I noticed that all his pictures had gone, save the odd one above the television. So sad, but the constant reminder of him was probably too much to bear. I had noticed when I called earlier that as soon as his name came up her voice would start to quiver and her eyes would well-up. I would change the subject quickly and get her onto the garden that she loved.

For the first time in the morning I was greeted with a big smile. "I have had a brain tumour so do not worry if I forget things when I am talking Alex."

"No problems! I forget most things anyway." I replied as I walked upstairs to her machine.

The machine was sitting patiently waiting for me. It was one of the last of the British Singers and in need of help. After a morning of fixing cheap *economy-engineered* bits of plastic it was nice to take something apart that was made by craftsmen that took pride in their work.

"Mrs Knight it is bad news I am afraid, both your main gears have broken and the other two look poor. To fix her is going to be a long job and expensive."

"Well Alex I shall do you a deal. You do trust me don't you?"

"Yes of course! What had you in mind?" I replied, a bit apprehensive. The morning had been long and bad and was probably about to get worse.

"If you repair my machine and do it for half of what the normal charge is I shall give you a surprise for repairing it that you will love."

I sat and thought. Images ran through my mind like *old clothes* or a *stale cake,* perhaps some over-ripe bananas that she could not eat? I'd had them all over the years. This was going to be a tricky deal to say the least. I could just see Yana scolding me again as I arrived home with yet another apron or tray of eggs instead of the all-important lubricant that eases the way through life – money.

"Well, as long as it will put a smile on my face, we have a deal." I said a bit apprehensively.

"Good! Good, now I will go and put the kettle on and I will make you a nice cup of coffee. Then I am going to tell you a story."

Mrs Knight disappeared and left me to start the tricky job of dismantling the lower part of the Singer in order to replace the gears. Some while later I heard her slow footsteps coming up the stairs. She walked into the room with a tray. The tray held a steaming cup of welcome coffee and a packet of McVitie's Rich Tea biscuits.

"Time for a break Alex," she said putting the tray down. I moved off my chair and let her sit on it as she looked like she needed the rest. When she recovered from her exertion she began her story.

"Back long before you were born I was already studying the ancient art of sewing. An art that has been with us since the earliest times. I was studying at the Sutton Art School. I was a young girl and war was raging all around us. I remember it as if it was yesterday. When the sirens started their horrible wail we would all rush out onto the green opposite the school and watch the German rockets streak overhead. Occasionally one would go silent. That was the scariest part, all the time they were screaming we were safe but as soon as they went silent then they would drop from the sky carrying death on their wings. We did not know if we would live until the end of the week let alone another year. Anyway, I am getting off my story, which I am still here to tell aren't I?" she said with a wry smile.

"After finishing my City & Guilds course, much to my mother's disapproval, I enlisted in the Women Auxiliary Air Force, the WAAF. At 17 I was in my uniform, which, due to my excellent training at the school, I made fit like a second skin. I worked in an office copying drawings and the like – for they had no such things in those days as photocopiers. Well, would you believe it, no sooner had I enrolled than VE – Victory in Europe – day was announced. I stayed on for another couple of years and had several wedding proposals. I said no to them all, packed my things and went home to my parents.

Before long I had met the man of my dreams and we moved into his parent's house for a year.

Then we found a newsagents and we lived above the shop and worked seven days a week running it. By the middle 1950s, for the first time, we had enough money for a holiday and a sewing machine. On that machine I made just about every stitch that we ever wore. I used it for 20 years before buying this one that you are fixing today."

As she talked I polished off the coffee and swallowed a couple of biscuits. Just a couple, mind, as I was on my never-ending-lifetime diet. Well, you just can't refuse peoples' hospitality! It would be an insult would it not? I had also nearly finished repairing the machine. While I put the finishing touches to the feed timing and tension she brought me up-to-date about the rest of her family.

All finished and the machine sewing as sweet a stitch as any ever made. I prepared myself for the *swap*. Off she went giggling.

"Now you are going to get something special!" I hear her say, her voice trailing away as she went down the corridor. My mind was doing wonders imagining all the rubbish that I was going to have to look pleased with. I wrote out the bill and cut the total in half. I thought that if I had already written it out it would not be so hard to accept the pair of socks she had just knitted or whatever it was.

Before long she was back in the room. Under her arm was a black box. In the box was a beautiful Singer 221k in simply stunning condition wrapped in polishing cloths. For a moment I was speechless. "I cannot accept this Mrs Knight, this is worth many times my bill – and so lovely."

"Nonsense Alex we made a deal and a deal is a deal. She was my baby, my pride and joy for half a century and now she is yours. I have not used her for 20 years so she will need a good service but I am sure she will make someone a very happy person."

"Mrs Knight I don't know what to say."

"Well, say nothing Alex I cannot use two machines but I know you will find a good home for her. Now off you go before you drive me mad with your mumbling."

As I left her house loaded with my tools, and her lovely machine safely tucked under my arm, the sun broke out from its hiding place and covered her front garden in a blaze of warm light. We both stopped for a second, in silence, soaking up the beautiful moment. "England in the sunshine is the most beautiful place God put on this earth Alex."

"That is for certain!" I said as I went down her path.

"It is not such a bad world really is it?" she said smiling.

"Mrs Knight, you sure got that right." I shouted back from the road.

My bad mood had disappeared. Like the weather, I had gone from a dull grey to bright day. One customer had thrown all the earlier bad ones away. I knew as I drove home for lunch and the wet roads steamed in the summer sunshine that Yana would be pleased. Probably for the first time that I had made a deal!

For once, in all these years, it was a real surprise. A beautiful Featherweight with a charming history from a lovely lady that could blow those blues away and looked on life as a blessing to be enjoyed with every breath she had.

SUN TRAP OF THE SOUTH

Eastbourne was bathing in glorious sunshine at the start of the visitors' season. Living up to her title of *Sun Trap of the South.*

The hotels were being dusted off and tables were being placed on the verandas for breakfast by the sea. Eastbourne (east of the river Bourne) has been around for many hundreds of years. The great fort of Pevensey still stands in proud witness of our Roman invaders 2000 years ago.

Eastbourne is primarily a tourist town made famous by the British royalty and their visits during the 19th and 20th century. I had the pleasure of meeting one of their maids when out on a call. She was a servant to George V while he convalesced here back in the 1930s.

She told me about the strict secrecy that surrounded his stay. How tea with salmon and cucumber sandwiches were served every day promptly at 4 pm. He would then take a brief walk around Gildredge Park before retiring.

I have even been in the house where he stayed. To fix a Singer Futura in the room he used. The machine belonged to a most elegant lady. The room remained almost untouched from the day the king left and it was like stepping back in time to a grander, more civilised world.

Because the weather was just so glorious I decided to take a short break from work and take the air. I walked along the seafront from the pier to the Lighthouse at Beachy Head. It is a long walk but the smell of the sea and the early morning sun on my back made the walk a delight.

As I got away from civilisation I stopped. While Rolly, my faithful mutt, chased seagulls from the rocks I absorbed the real essence of the day.

The barnacles on the rocks were clicking, sounding like applause drifting out from a distant theatre. The sea was lapping gently at the sand and the sun was sparkling like diamonds as it danced on the tips of the waves below the new dawn sky. Eastbourne can look distinctly Mediterranean in the sun.

In the distance fishing boats from the harbour were heading for the rocks off Beachy Head hoping to find the first run of the summer bass. The smell was pure heaven. A cool salty smell of fresh seaweed and nature was carried on the warm south-westerly breeze.

About an hour of hopping over weed-covered rocks where little pools of sea-life were captured from the retreating tide took me to the huge red-and-white-striped lighthouse. It was built around the turn of the 20th century to warn sailors of the dangers lying beneath the sea at this outcrop of land. Many ships have run aground and the crew perished in the cold waters off Beachy Head.

The English Channel is said to be the busiest shipping lane in the world.

I looked up at the awesome face of the white cliffs. The top perfectly trimmed with a grass edge, like a massive white duvet piped in green. There stands Devil's Chimney, hundreds of feet of sheer cliff. This is a notorious suicide spot where many a life has ended. While it is a morbid spot it is also one of the most beautiful places on earth to die.

I sat for a while and let Rolly frolic around on the sand. When we were children my parents would bring us to this special place, our secret beach, for picnics. A patch of sand in the rocks, a hidden lagoon, a touch of paradise far away from anyone. Since, nudists have taken over the beach and in high summer, prance about like peacocks, in more ways than one. When I was younger I often wanted to take a catapult and hide amongst the rocks and give them some schoolboy humour right on their bare bums.

After a short rest I headed homeward and took an old fisherman's path up the cliffs to a grassy track that runs along the base of the downs. I stopped for a while to exchange good mornings with a fox that sprang out of nowhere. He looked at me as if I was trespassing and was not a bit afraid of Rolly. How dare I interrupt his hunt for breakfast!

Golden threads of dew-soaked gossamer were floating up the valley from spiders that had been busy during the night. As they drifted past they caught the morning light, shimmering silently on their way to nowhere.

The fox would have been after a rabbit because the downs are home to millions of rabbits ever since the Romans or Normans brought them here for their tables. As I walked back the sun was warming up and butterflies were starting their daily hunt for nectar among the mass of downland flowers. A rare Sussex Blue butterfly flitted along the path as I walked. The soft grass cushioning my feet with every step.

As I drew nearer to civilisation I came to my old school. Children's voices drifted up on the gentle breeze. The echoes of kids playing, sounding like a swimming pool full of people enjoying themselves. What a great place to have a school. How lucky I was to play hockey, rugby and cricket there on the downland turf and to learn about life while gazing out the school windows at the sea.

Lucky too, to be learning poetry while the curtains in the upstairs dormitories of our school billowed in and out pushed from a wild sea wind. Where our headmaster would often read aloud from poems like *The Highwayman* as we sat wide-eyed watching him perform.

> *The wind was a torrent of darkness among the gusty trees,*
> *The moon was a ghostly galleon tossed upon cloudy seas,*
> *The road was a ribbon of moonlight over the purple moor,*
> *And the highwayman came riding – riding – riding – riding –*
> *The highway man came riding, up to the old inn-door.*

By the time I got back to my car Eastbourne was coming to life. A few people had started to move. The local newsagents were busy delivering papers. The milkman rattled past me, bottles clinking in the milk float. The postman had stopped to chat with the man I had passed prawning on the beach. They were both examining his catch, peering down admiringly into a plastic shopping-bag full of prawns. Later they would be boiling in a pot with seaweed and a few bay leaves for flavour.

I made my way home to open the post and start another day. There was a whole pile of machines to service and repair. The usual bunch of mail to open. The closure of our local Singer shop, after 70 years, had put even more work on my plate.

As I got to our gate the first cloud of the day floated past. I headed indoors and put the coffee on. It would be a busy day.

Michelham Priory, ancient and beautiful set in Abbotts Wood which was mentioned in the Domesday book. It was formerly an Augustinian priory.

Sussex lambs on the Pevensey marshes. These sturdy sheep survive harsh winters and are built for it.

*The Devonshire Park Theatre
where we have spent many an
afternoon watching plays in the
wonderful Victorian theatre.*

*One of the last remaining
Martello Towers in original
condition. Built to protect our
shores from nasty Napoleon
they were also used to test the
power of artillery. As a young
man, my friend and I tried to
buy this tower. I would still
love it. One of the last
untouched towers it is set into
history like a full stop.
Napoleon – the bogey man
never made it across the
channel.*

The famous meandering river Cuckmere covered in snow

Harvest time on the South Downs is a magical time

THE CHIEF

On one of my calls I came across a retired couple living in a very posh area of my hometown. Eastbourne is famous for two things. Jokes about old people and Beachy Head. Many people retire to the *Sun Trap of the South*. Eastbourne not only has an old population, which I love, but also more old women per head than any other place in the country. Whether it is the clean air or chalky water that promotes this is anyone's guess.

Beachy Head is not only famous for its breath-taking beauty but also as the number one suicide spot in the country! Many weeks our local paper tells stories of these tragic endings but it is also common for passers-by to help a depressed or suicidal person back from their 600-foot final step and become heroes.

I once came across a very unhappy middle-aged woman trying to ram her car over the edge of the cliff. I talked to her until her husband came. I didn't help much. Two weeks later she accomplished her last mission.

I digress, back to the story. In their youth this couple had been scientific explorers. On one of their early journeys they had travelled to South America in search of untouched civilisations. They had planned to travel up the Amazon until they had left civilisation behind. Then they could explore the wilderness and examine local tribes in their own surroundings living off the forest.

Everything went to plan. They took with them some things to trade with the people such as beads, mirrors and other trinkets. They set out up the Amazon from their base and headed west into the unknown.

The going was slow and travelling up river hard in the humid atmosphere where insects loved the fresh soft meat of these new mobile meals. They noted many different fauna and flora as they went. Their guides helped with the local names. Flocks of blue and yellow Macaws called to each other overhead while giant electric-blue Morph butterflies flitted in front of their canoes.

In their dugouts they passed Inca ruins that had lain dormant for centuries untouched by man. Sights of the virgin Amazon rain forest filled their waking hours. At night the sounds of the Amazon came to life as huge bats circled the campfire and strange calls floated through the forest canopy.

After many days they came upon the first village of native Amazonians. They were filled with expectation and excitement as their canoes pulled up at a makeshift jetty. This was their first meeting with a real native tribe. Had they even seen explorers before? Would they be eaten for supper? With their Leica cameras and fists full of goodies they made their way up to the village.

The villagers were all gathered in the centre of the village and were engaged in some kind of meeting. Much to their surprise the villagers paid little attention to them. They seemed engrossed in the goings on at the centre of the circle.

As they edged their way to the circle there, in the middle, was the chief of the tribe. He was a stocky man, half-naked, with a piece of brightly coloured cloth wrapped around him and beads around his neck. To their utter astonishment he was having a sewing-machine demonstration.

Yes, it's the truth. A salesman was demonstrating a hand-crank Singer. He was there to exchange machines for native goods that he, in turn, sold to tourists to make money. Almost dumbstruck our explorers approached the chief to talk to him but they were politely signalled to wait.

Later the man was granted an audience with the big man and was summoned into a large hut. His wife had to wait outside because no women were allowed inside.

The hut was sparsely furnished with a fire in the centre, its smoke trailing upward towards a hole in the ceiling. A few ornaments were hanging from the roof beams. The chief motioned him to come forward and sit. They shared a drink of an unknown, bitter-tasting, liquid that burnt his throat and set his stomach on fire but left him with a satisfied feeling.

Through his guide he tried to converse with the chief. He asked questions about the wildlife and the villager's ways of living. The chief paid little notice so he showed the goodies that he had brought. The chief examined them, pausing for a while to play with a mirror while muttering to himself. Then, taking a row of beads and placing them over his head, the chief said something to the guide, rose to his feet, and walked out of the hut without so much of a sideways glance.

It was the last time they saw the chief.

Somewhat bemused at the whole affair, "Well, what did the chief say?" asked our explorer of his guide.

"Chief say, tell man to bring Singers. Then we talk about wildlife."

Eastbourne Heritage Centre is well worth a visit and holds much of Eastbourne's history.

NANCY'S STORY

Customers were phoning in every day. Money was building in the bank. Busy though business was we managed to escape for a break.

We had a glorious holiday sailing 500 miles up the Nile and visiting the Pyramids at Giza, last of the Seven Wonders of the World. On the first day of my long-awaited holiday I pulled open the curtains in my berth expecting to see the wonderful Nile. You know the sort of thing. Ibis flying past and feluccas gliding down river with their sails full of warm desert air.

Instead I was confronted with a Juki industrial sewing machine – nice! A boat had pulled up along side us in the night and I was right opposite the ship's repairman who was busily repairing tablecloths. Even on holiday I could not escape from work!

All my hard work had been paying off and my reputation was growing fast – for my ability with sewing machines, that is. I had managed to buy a real car instead of the van that had served us well the past few years.

The day I picked up my new car I felt like a king. The smell of a new car is something so special. It was the first big reward from my business. I did not help things by cracking a couple of ribs shortly afterwards.

I fell off my son's bike. I was being stupid. The wheelie was great. It is just the ending where I fell onto the handlebars that needs a little work. Mind you, all of Tom's friends watching had the best laugh of the year.

Cracked ribs were no reason to slow down so I carried on bravely in silence for the next few weeks as they healed. The saying, *It only hurts when I laugh,* certainly came home to me.

Bold, brave and bruised I carried on with work and knocked on Nancy Ravenhall's door. While I was busy repairing her machine she told me all about her father who had been in the sewing trade.

During the first World War Nancy's father was a young man on lookout-duty in the trenches. A sniper's bullet exploded in his back and, during the ensuing attack, he was left behind enemy lines. He crawled three miles on his belly before collapsing. Sometime later a parson was blessing the dead and passed him by before realising that he was alive.

He was rushed to the field hospital and operated on. Once he could be moved he was shipped home for a further 16 back operations at a specialist unit. He was then placed in a convalescent home.

This is where the sewing machines come in. Before the war he was a builder but now his back held bits of a German dumdum bullet and he was unable to return to his old way of life. During the three years he spent recovering at the hospital he was trained as a tailor. He was taught by the best and went to work in a top London gentleman's outfitters.

He made suits and shirts but his real strength was his waistcoats. They became renowned. As his reputation grew men travelled from across the country to have him make a bespoke waistcoat.

There were two of her father's stories that stood out for Nancy. The first was about a suit that he made for a man with a deformed back. After Henry had finished the suit, seven fittings later, when the man put it on he looked as straight as a Beefeater at the Palace. All the special padding and cutting had paid off. It was with great pride that he held open the shop door as the customer walked out into 1930s London.

The other was a special waistcoat made for an Arab prince who liked to gamble in the London nightclubs. It was pure mustard Cashmere on the front and cream silk behind. The buttons down the front were brought in by special courier from Hatton Gardens. They were 3-carat diamonds, six of them, in gold casings.

That waistcoat is probably hanging in a wardrobe somewhere, right now, owned by someone who won it on a roll of the dice. I can just imagine that smoke-filled London nightclub half a century ago and those diamonds glinting in the gambler's eyes.

The other funny incident that Nancy told me about was when she went to a country fair with her dad. They were walking over to the coconut stalls at the fair when Henry spotted one of the female seamstresses that worked with him. He went over and introduced his daughter, Nancy.

The girl was wearing a beautiful blouse that was the latest in fashion at the time. When Nancy asked about it the girl blushed. She made Nancy promise to keep it a secret. The girl worked for the great London firm of Norman Hartnell. One day she had crept up to the cutting room in her lunch break and copied a pattern that was lying on the table. She placed her newspaper over it and made an exact duplicate of the blouse. Then she got hold of some silk lining that had been replaced from the inside of a mink coat.

At home she had made up the silk blouse but never dared to wear it out. If she had been caught it would have meant instant dismissal. The reason was that the pattern she had copied was very special. It had been commissioned for none other than Princess Margaret.

She was dying to wear it and thought that she would be safe at a country fair far away from the city. Nancy kept her little secret and the girl not only wore the very special blouse but also a big smile as she floated around the summer fair.

Nancy said that most of her father's work was done by hand, especially the collars and the buttonholes. His golden rule was always to baste twice and sew once. He had a Bradbury treadle machine all of his tailoring life. He maintained it himself and in over 35 years, it never once went wrong.

Bradburys were one of the pioneers in the British sewing machine field having been founded in the 1850s. My favourite is the Bradbury Wellington because it has a picture of the Duke of Wellington boldly emblazoned on the front bed. At their Manchester works they also made baby carriages and bicycles.

Nancy sews on a 60s Singer 416 that needed a new gear and a service and that is how I came to hear all about her father. I am sure her machine will last another decade or so.

I asked her what had happened to the Bradbury. Sadly it bit the dust when she could not get needles and it was thrown away. What a pity I was not there to catch it!

Part of my collection that has been growing for years

An officer stands guard on the seafront in Eastbourne. The 2nd Royal Sussex Regiment fought campaigns all over the world including the Boer war in South Africa.

ONE OF THOSE DAYS

There are days when everything that can go wrong, does. They say things come in threes. Well, on this day they did!

I started as normal and headed out of Eastbourne to my first call in Bexhill-on-Sea. When I arrived the old dear had lost the key to her sewing machine case. No problem, with a little dexterity and the patience of a safe cracker the lid popped open. The Singer 28 shuttle machine was soon sewing like new. I packed my tools and sped off to my next call.

I knocked on the door to be greeted by a woman leaning out of the sitting room window. She told me she was locked in the room. It turned out that her husband had painted the door and had not put the handle back on. As she went into the room, her four-year-old son pushed the door closed behind, locking them both in.

There was no way out and she had been there an hour waiting for someone to find her. I went into action again. Round the back to the garden gate. With the agility of a one-legged carthorse I managed to get over it while putting a neat tear in a most humiliating position in my trousers.

However, I was not deterred, through the back door and in to work on the sitting room door. Within a few seconds the door opened and a beaming little boy was smiling at me. He looked so pleased, as if I had come to play for the day.

I fixed her Pfaff Industrial quickly and hit the road. I was a bit the worse for wear and walking rather cautiously to cover a slightly breezy area now opened to the elements.

At my next call I was working away like a busy little bee, kneeling down to hide my ripped trousers. I had the help of a Heinz 57 mongrel dog sitting beside me as I worked away. I was adjusting the bobbin case tension screw when it dropped out. I caught a glimpse of it as it bounced off the table and fell onto the dog.

What was the chance of that happening? Just what I needed and running late as well!

Now, normally, I can find these little screws, no problem. But the dog was not co-operating. She was convinced I wanted to play. I had to get her owner to hold her as I stroke her coat, feeling for the screw. The owner is convinced I was mad and the dog was lapping up all the attention, slobbering all over me.

In the end she had a brainwave and we used her husband's comb on the dog. After a few strokes out popped the screw. Much to the astonishment of the woman and delight of the dog that ran around the house as if it was possessed. What a commotion!

I was running about one hour late but had to stop in Hastings at a public convenience to answer the call of nature. This was where the third and final obstacle happened. In the loo was a burst pipe. I did not pay much attention to it. No sooner was I about my business than the outside door slammed shut!

What the…?

My mind was now racing as I heard the lock being engaged. Not being in a position to get to the door at that exact moment I started to shout. I then rushed to the door and proceeded to hammer on it like mad. I was locked in the town bog for the rest of the day with a burst pipe for company. Not my idea of a good time!

I had no tools and no way out.

To my rescue came a rather bewildered-looking council worker, "Where the hell did you come from mate?" he asked.

"Eastbourne," I replied as I passed him scratching his head.

I had the distinct feeling he was staring straight at the rip in my butt as I walked back to the car. I just kept a stiff upper lip and quickened my step. Glad to be extracted from my watery prison I headed off wet and worn, back home. I had just about had enough for the morning.

When I got home my wife asked me if I had had a good morning.

"Don't ask," I said, "but have you still got that invisible repair patch and some clean trousers"?

It was just one of those days.

SLASH

"Alex, where on earth have you been? You look like you have been dragged through a hedge backwards!" Jessie laughed, leaning over the closed-lower part of her stable style front door.

"Jose Miguel's, the upholsterers in Blackboys. His big Mauser over lock machine had gone wrong." I said brushing off a few more duck feathers. "He is a superb upholsterer but his workshop is always like a turkey factory before Christmas. I feel like I have been tarred and feathered."

"Well you won't be able to walk down the high street like that! People will be talking you know." Jessie said brushing me off on her porch. "Pillow feathers all over you. Heaven knows what folks will think! Now come on in I have locked Slash in the kitchen until you are in and settled. You know how he does like to play."

Play? Play! That dog was the Devil's spawn. A ferocious Jack Russell who looked at all men as if they were fair game. He was called Slash because he'd sustained a nasty cut along his back as a puppy. I fancied that it was his mother, trying to kill him before he could grow into the little monster that he had become.

I had learned many years before about Slash and the golden rule was never to take your eyes off the beast. Especially when you were vacating the premises! That was his favourite time to have a chunk out of your ankle or bum. Fixing Jessie's sewing machine was usually a breeze but the dog was another matter altogether. He had drawn blood before and would not hesitate to try again given the slightest opportunity.

I plonked my tools down beside the Husqvarna sewing machine that had developed a fault in the electronic panel that controls the automatic needle positioning. Although Jessie was pushing 70 she always had advanced sewing machines. She had learned as a child that quality in sewing machines pays if you are to make your living from them. With machines like the Husky 6570E I have to become more of an electronics expert than a sewing machine engineer.

Jessie had come down to Sussex as a young woman during the Second World War to work on the farms. As a Land girl, she was one of the unseen thousands who had helped keep the larders stocked during those lean years. After the war Jessie could not bring herself to leave Sussex and its miles of open farmland. Her love affair with this beautiful county meant she would not be parted from it.

I opened my toolbox, sat in the chair, and stayed perfectly still, waiting for Slash's release.

"Ready?" Jessie called from the kitchen door.

"As I'll ever be, I suppose," I replied reluctantly.

With that Jessie opened the door and the snarling beast ran into the room like a mini charging bull. He made straight for the front door passing me at full speed, his little legs a blur. At the door he sniffed and growled. I almost expected the beast to say, "Fee fie foe fum I smell the blood of an English man!"

The terrier slowly but surely followed my trail zigzagging up the corridor right up to my feet. As he arrived he looked up for a split second, no more, there was a touch of shock in his beady black eyes. I smiled nervously and lifted my hand to stroke him but he snapped at my fingers.

"Slash, you naughty boy you'll be the death of me," Jessie said, marching across the room. She reached down and clasped her hands each side of his overstuffed belly, like a huge crane, lifting the creature. She cuddled the dog and brought him closer to me. I smiled, he snarled.

"No change there then?" I said shrugging my shoulders.

"Its not you, Alex. He likes you, but he never has liked other men. Last week he chased the UPS deliveryman right up to the village. It is not his fault, the little darling – I am sure he was mistreated as a puppy."

He would be mistreated now if I had any choice, I thought. My boot up his backside would be a start.

"Never mind," I said. "I'm sure you're right, he likes me really. Normally I get on very well with animals but Slash seems to have a bit of an attitude problem."

Jessie sat in her chair opposite me and held him as I worked. Each time I glanced up towards him a snarl came back, quickly accompanied by a telling off from Jessie followed by a cuddle and a stroke. She referred to

Slash as Sweetheart. I could not imagine the little beast being anyone's sweetheart but who was I to judge as long as I did not have to live with him.

In no time, I had soldered a new capacitor and was busy servicing the sewing machine. Jessie had taken Slash into the kitchen with her while she was making coffee. The phone rang.

"Jessie the phone is ringing!" I called.

"Get it for me would you Alex?"

I picked up the receiver, "Hello–?" I listened for a moment.

"Jessie, its Meals on Wheels! They want to know if you would prefer beef or pork for your lunch?"

"Ask for beef Alex," said Jessie, and then she whispered, "Slash prefers the beef."

I ordered Jessie's and – from the sound of it – Slash's lunch and then drank my coffee. All the time under the steely gaze of the black-eyed monster. As long as Jessie had him under control I was fine but leaving the grounds was another problem altogether.

It became a joint operation for as I made movements to go the dog sensed that it was time to taste the blood of the sewing machine repairman. He started to wriggle and spit in Jessie's arms. Jessie held firm in her armchair. "You had better go now while I still have strength to hold the little dear."

"No need to tell me twice Jessie I will see myself out. Just don't let go!" I made a sharp march down the long hall to the front door.

The lower part of the door was closed and the upper part open against the wall. As I got to the door I heard the awful scrambling sound of little legs on the carpet. I looked around in horror to see a streak of teeth rushing headlong down the corridor at a hundred mile an hour. Slash had the look of death in his eyes.

I scrambled out of the house but by the time I put my toolbox down the beast was upon me. Born from years of practice the dog had managed to squeeze through an impossible gap as I slammed the door shut. Both the dog and I were now outside the house. He had shot past me, ears pinned back, mouth snarling as I twisted like a Spanish matador. Slash made a wide circle over the lawn like a Spitfire coming around for another attack. I was trapped. I stepped back from my toolbox until my back pressed against the door frame. In the second or so before Slash made his attack my mind was buzzing. I crouched like a sumo wrestler, as prepared as I could be.

He launched at me. A lump of slithering slobbering sinew with one thing on his mind, *bite Alex*. The dog cleared my toolbox, in retrospect almost gracefully given his stubby legs. What I would have given for a cricket bat! I would have gone for a six and watched Slash disappear over the boundary, howling all the way.

In his enthusiasm to taste meat, he had made one fateful mistake. He misjudged the distance between my toolbox and my legs. Slash landed before he reached me and stumbled.

This tiny mistake gave me the chance I needed. I pinned the little monster down under my bent knee. I grabbed the scruff of his neck with a grip of iron. In one movement, I rose, twisted and threw the gnashing beast back over the half door into the hallway of the house. I laughed with triumph.

Not a scratch! I could not believe it! I peeked over the door and lurched back as Slash made an attempt to rip my throat out.

"Tough luck you little – Oh! Hello Jessie, you got here just in time. It looks like Slash is getting a little frustrated." I said with a big smirk over my face.

Jessie picked up Slash and told him off in the sweetest way while he snarled at me.

"Whatever will we do with you Slash? You really will be the death of me one day!"

I waved, picked up my toolbox and walked down the path with a little skip in my step.

I never saw Slash again. He was last seen chasing a gypsy-tipping lorry down Slugwash Lane near Newick. I can only imagine that he is happy now sitting around the campfire along some old highway with a band of gypsies, eating hedgehogs – that gypsies refer to as hedge pigs and are apparently very tasty – and growling at unsuspecting tax inspectors who occasionally come-a-calling.

I was still thinking about Slash when my next customer broke my thoughts.

"Magnet! Keep away from Alex's toolbox you little monster" Shouted Nicky as she came running over to her son.

"Why on earth do you call him Magnet?" I asked just boiling with curiosity.

"Why! I'll show you why! Ben open your hands and show them to me!"

Ben rolled opened his sticky little fingers and to my amazement there was a handful of my screws and three machine take up springs. I had not even noticed him bend over my toolbox.

I looked straight at Ben. "No wonder they call you magnet." I said as I prised my bits and pieces out of his hands.

Ben just smiled innocently back at me with that wide eyed gaze that only three year olds can master. He then ran off to play havoc with his Alsatian that was trying to sleep under the table. I got back down to work but was soon interrupted again.

"I have done a pardon me." Said the little girl that had wobbled up to me in her nappy.

"A what?" I asked

"A pardon me." She repeated giggling and sucking her finger.

I stopped work and tried to think what the child could possibly mean. All suddenly became clear as liquid, stink rushed up my nostrils causing every muscle in my face to contort in the most hideous way. Only a nappy overflowing with well-digested baby food could fill a room with such an unpleasant odour in so short a time.

The Alsatian slunk out of the room in a sheepish fashion as if he were the culprit. I looked down at the nappy that was wobbling like an over ripe water melon about to burst. The only difference being what was about to come out of her elasticated leg bands of the nappy was no sweet substance.

"Nicky! Nicky!" I shouted my voice rising a little in despair. "Your daughter has a little present for you I just have to get a part from the car."

I did not stop for an answer, Magnet could eat half my toolbox and pinch the rest, I needed fresh air. Gasping I ran outside and sat on the garden wall for a few moments before shuffling around in the back of my car pretending to look for something. I waited a good five minutes before returning.

On arriving in the lounge I found the smelly girl was wrapped in a nice new nappy and leaping on the sofa. Magnet was pulling hair out of the Alsatian that had crept back to its place under the table and all the windows were open. Normality had returned.

"Find what you were looking for?" Nicky asked with a very suspicious look.

"Yep, no problem just a little piece I needed that's all." I lied, not looking her in the eye in case I got that *all you men are the same look*. I got back down to fixing her Huskylock machine but kept a keen eye on both Magnet and his sister. I glanced over at the dog who was looking straight at me as if to say, think yourself lucky I have to put up with this every day, you're just visiting.

I could not help wondering how many times the poor dog had got the blame for the kids smells, he certainly had the crawling out of the room bit down to a fine art.

Before long I found myself waving goodbye to the kids thinking how no day was ever the same in my work as a travelling repairman. My next call was interesting and the lady had a wonderful tale of how she had obtained her Singer model 15k from her old school headmistress. I tried to remember what she was telling me but it was no good. All I could think of was Magnet – with his sticky little fingers and his sister waddling up to me saying that she had done a pardon-me!

Simply priceless.

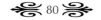

Working on my old Myford Super 7 is always a pleasure. Here I am milling the final slot which is a piece for a Singer 45K. I often have to make parts for obsolete machines to keep them running.

The finished machine sewing beautifully with my special modification. Four dealers told the customer her machine was obsolete and irrepairable.

SHORTCUT

I have many customers a few miles down the coast in the quaint old seaside town of Bexhill-on-Sea.

Bexhill was the first place in England to have a car race. That was over 100 years ago and it is still held each year. It is a stone's throw from where that Norman upstart called William landed in 1066 and made us all eat Brie and radishes for a few hundred years.

One of these customers, Bev Beasley, works for the local dry cleaners as a machinist doing customer's alterations. One day a pretty Italian woman in her 40s came into the shop and asked for a skirt to be made shorter. Alan the boss, took the skirt, Bev shortened it and the next week the woman came to collect it.

"It needs to be a little shorter," she said.

Well the skirt was already quite short, so Alan told her to see Bev, who was a bit concerned that the woman wanted another inch off the skirt, that was already so short it was barely decent. However she marked the skirt at the exact spot and duly carried out her orders.

In conversation with the woman it turned out the skirt, which was leather, was for the Christmas office party and she wanted to be the centre of attention of the young men of the office. Bev finished the skirt and gave it to Alan. He remarked that it was closer to a belt than a skirt.

All went well, the woman picked the skirt up with a big smile. Job done – or so Bev thought – because all hell was about to break loose.

A week later a red-faced man walked into the shop and demanded to see the manager. It was the husband, "What is the meaning of this?" he demanded holding up the belt, sorry, skirt.

Alan was a bit taken aback by the husband's ferocity and asked him to explain. Apparently the husband was woken at three in the morning to find his wife returning home after her Christmas party wearing the short leather skirt. He demanded to know what was going on. What was she doing wearing something so outrageous, at her age, at a party full of young men, especially one to which he was not invited!

The woman, in a panic, told him that she had taken the skirt in to the cleaners and they had cut too much off the hem. As she had picked the skirt up on the same day as the party she had no time to find something different and just had to wear the skirt.

The outraged husband did not want to hear Alan's explanation so Bev was called to back him up. The husband was hearing none of this. His hot Italian blood got the better of him and he started to rant and rave. His sweet little wife would never do anything like that. Alan's only course of action was to call the police. The boys in blue arrived and dragged him out of the shop screaming, "I will see you all in court."

That is exactly what did happen. The pretty wife would not admit to having the skirt made too short. Alan and Bev would not apologise for something they were told to do, so off to court they all went.

The day of the case arrived and they all attended court. Things ran rather more swiftly than expected and it became clear to all, including the husband, the truth of the matter. Before an hour was up the judge had stopped proceedings and thrown the case out. He summed up by telling the woman to try to grow up and act her age. He told her husband to calm down. He also noted that it was rather unwise for her to come to his court in a skirt three inches above her knees.

So, a little adjustment on a leather skirt had caused uproar in the local community and everyone had a good gossip. The couple have not been seen out together since. In fact the last time they were seen together was the day of the trial as they disappeared from court shouting at each other in Italian.

BABIES AND BLUSHES

Sussex had become like a bathtub with the tap left on. The ground was sodden from weeks of rain. It just could not absorb any more water. The most rain since records began had flooded country, towns and villages alike.

The damage had been estimated at four thousand million pounds. Yes, that's right, four thousand million. The earth and the sky that was normally in harmony was having a hard time and more storm clouds were rolling in from the coast.

I drove near to the ancient town of Alfriston. It is a stone's throw from the Berwick Church that was decorated by the famous Bloomsbury Group. They were staying, at the time, at Charleston Farmhouse not far from the church.

Alfriston was unreachable by car. The beautiful Sussex town, so popular with the tourists, had been hit hard by flooding. The Cuckmere valley, that normally had a little river meandering through it, was now an inland sea. You had to see it to believe it!

In the early morning glow it looked like a scene from an African flood plain. I am making no more jokes about Noah for the moment.

It was back in the great storm of 1987 that we last saw similar devastation. That time it was the wind that caused the chaos. Fifteen million trees were uprooted in Southern England. Huge swathes of woodland were destroyed.

There were positive sides. Bluebells flourished in the newly opened woods and boar that had escaped from several farms bred over the following years. All this seemed to take East Sussex back to a more pleasant era. I for one love the idea of these huge beasts roaming around foraging in our ancient woodlands. Mind you, it might give the local dog owners a bit of a scare if they came across one in the woods.

Woodpeckers were also benefiting from the fallen trees that had become infested with bugs as they rot. I have seen more woodpeckers these last few years since '87 than ever before.

At my first call of the morning I found Mrs Croft busily shovelling up the molehills in her garden into her bucket.

"Best soil you'll ever come across," she chirped happily to me as I arrived. "I never complain when they come-a-calling and leave me my potting compost for the year," she added heaping more soil into the bucket.

I followed her into the back porch as she swapped her Wellingtons for a pair of old slippers that seemed to almost leap on her feet. The smell of bacon was heavy in the air and in the kitchen, her husband was busily champing away at his breakfast. I had a sudden hunger and tried hard not to stare like a starving child at Mr Croft's breakfast.

The Crofts run a pig farm and before long, I was being given the low-down on the best bacon.

"Make sure you always buy dry-cured sweet-smoked bacon, you will love it," said Mr Croft as he finished off the last slice on his plate with a swig from his teacup. "None of this fast, sugar-water, prepared stuff they sell nowadays. It's more water than bacon," he grunted with a note of disapproval.

No sooner had he finished than he pulled on his wellies and disappeared out the back door touching his cap with two fingers and nodding goodbye as he went. "Happy pigs make great bacon," he laughed as he closed the door.

Mrs Croft worked for Singers in the 1960s. She was a sales girl and demonstrator. It was a large shop up in Nottingham with five salesmen. At her retirement, as a present, she could pick any machine in the store. What did she choose? It was a Singer 99.

She could have had so many different machines but she chose one of the most simple and reliable. It paid off because my call was the first in 36 years. Funny thing though, she nearly picked a 222k Featherweight. She decided against it because she was doing curtains at the time and wanted something heavier. I didn't tell her the price difference on the machines today!

Once I had finished she packed me off with a pound of best bacon wrapped in some old newspaper. I left her pulling on her wellies and heading back to her molehills.

I still laugh when I think of her. I have absolutely no memory of what machine I fixed at her house. It's all blank except for her and that dressing gown!

Alfriston High Street probably one of the prettiest streets in England.

A beautiful winter scene in the Sussex countryside, near Abbotts Wood, Hailsham.
The oak tree was so prolific in the area it was nicknamed The Sussex Weed.

SYLVIA'S MOTHER

Sylvia was the typical silver-haired old lady with horn-rimmed spectacles and a bright bubbly face. She showed me to the machine, a 1920s Frister & Rossmann.

"My mother bought that brand new to make my clothes as a child," she announced as I sat down to repair it.

The problem with the basic shuttle machine was that it kept jamming in a certain position. I started to work my way through from the top right hand side down to the main shaft and along to the shuttle area. I could not find the problem and I kept rocking the machine backward and forward to locate the jam.

I took the left side-plate above the needle off and carried on rocking. I found the jam. A small washer had somehow dropped into a position where it was hitting the needle bar on its downward stroke.

"I think I have found your problem Mrs Wilkinson," I said as I reached in with my trusty bent-tip tweezers to remove the washer. I slowly prised the oily piece of metal out of the Frister & Rossmann and dropped it on the table with a satisfied ting like a surgeon dropping a removed bullet into a bowl.

I took a sip of tea that had been sitting waiting for me to finish and glanced at the washer. It looked unusual. I picked it up with one hand and rubbed it between my thumb and forefinger.

"You know, I think this is a coin," I said and, on further rubbing with a cloth, a rather sad and battered looking sixpence appeared.

"I can see the date, it is 1935," I said holding it up to the light from the window. Sylvia went all quiet and, as I looked at her, I saw a little smile appear and her eyes widen.

"You know, I put that sixpence in there over 60 years ago," she said.

Sylvia, as a young girl, had sneaked into her parents' bedroom while they

89

were downstairs. She wanted to see what her mum was making for her. Once at the machine she saw the sixpence on the table. Without thinking she picked it up and slipped it into the slot by the take-up lever of the machine.

"It looked just like the slot in my money box," Sylvia sniggered. "Acting on impulse, as kids do, I simply dropped it in. No sooner had I done it than I had forgotten all about it, until now."

That sixpence had sat there for six decades while the world turned. Then, one day, it had decided to jam itself into the needle-bar assembly.

"Well that's one valuable coin," I said.

"Why?" she replied.

"Well it might have been only worth sixpence when you put it in your mum's machine but you have just paid me fifteen quid to get it back!"

We both had a laugh and I finished servicing the old machine. I left her holding the sixpence.

I am sure that as I turned to leave I caught a glimpse, behind those horn-rimmed spectacles, of that little girl who had snuck into her parents' bedroom all those years ago.

Old Town, Eastbourne. St. Mary's Church and the Coach-house were built in the 12th century. The pub and the church were the centre of village life in England.

WHOOPS

Everyone makes mistakes and, on this day, so did I. The only difference with my mistake was that it had quite an effect on Hailsham council.

Many moons ago Mrs Bennett, called me to repair her machine. The usual scenario but, because she worked every day, it was difficult to organise a time for me to call when she was at home. So we arranged for me to call at her place of work, the Hailsham Council offices.

Hailsham is a quaint little market town with one of the oldest markets in England. It is protected from development by the order of an ancient king, hundreds of years ago.

I arrived on schedule and she took me to an out-of-the-way room at the very top of the building. There, waiting for my attention, was a pretty Harris No 9 that had been converted from a hand-crank to electric. I started to work on the machine.

Things were going well and within a short time the machine was repaired and serviced. All I needed to do was balance the tensions. I searched for a wall-socket and found one in the corner of the room. Older buildings like that rarely have more than one electrical outlet per room. Although there was a plug in the socket it did not seem to lead anywhere, in fact it went straight into the floor!

I unplugged it, put the Harris in, and continued to set the tensions. After a short time I became aware of a commotion coming from downstairs. There was a lot of shouting and running around. I stopped to look out of the window thinking there might be a fire or an accident in the street below but I could see nothing. So I continued with my work. The commotion kept on and on and seemed to be getting closer.

Suddenly the door crashed open and a red-faced bull of a man came charging in. He stared around looking for something and then to my astonishment he went for the plug that I had removed. He ripped out the Harris plug and put the original one back in.

"How long has that bloody plug been out?" he demanded in a strained high-pitched almost-hysterical whine.

"About 20 minutes," I replied thinking I had better not retort with some humorous quip as I usually do.

He looked far too upset to antagonise further and I might have ended up being thrown to my death from the upstairs window.

"Do you realise you have shut down the entire council's computer system?"

My jaw dropped. I said nothing as it dawned on me the seriousness of my predicament. Thoughts of lawsuits raced round my head. Pictures of me in the dock at the local magistrates' court, with a hundred murderous council employees pointing at me and sneering, sprung to mind. I also thought of queues of pensioners waiting for their pensions only to be shown a poster of me!

Before I could reply he had disappeared. I stood as if in shock for a few moments scanning the floor to see if he had left any hoof-marks as he charged out of the room. Quietly I finished off my work thinking there was no way out of the building except past all the office workers. I did peek out of the window to see if a fire escape would mercifully appear but no such luck.

As I packed my tools to leave I heard footsteps on the stairway outside the room. I glanced around for somewhere to hide but, too late, the door opened and in came the same man. This time he had a normal complexion, no red face and no steam from his nostrils – surely I must have imagined that.

"No damage done old chap," he said in a soft upper class British accent.

Had he been away to boarding school in the last ten minutes? I thought, because his manner had improved so dramatically, *perhaps they run compact elocution classes at the Council.*

"We put the plug in this room because no body ever comes in here so we knew it would not be unplugged." he said.

"I am ever so sorry I had no idea it was for your computers," I replied feeling relieved. Then in true self-employed style I seized upon his temporary good nature and passed him the invoice for the sewing machine repair, "Could you see that Mrs Bennett gets this?" I requested.

He did not rip it up. In fact he went and got payment straight away, probably aware of the shock he had given me earlier. I then put my head down and tried to get out of the Council offices as quietly as a church mouse. As I glanced up nearing the door not a soul was watching me. They all had their heads buried in their computer screens.

So I lived to fight another day I thought as the bright sunlight of freedom fell on my face.

Now, before I unplug anything at a customer's house I always ask where it goes, remembering the face of *Mr Bull* as I now call him.

In the Friston Church graveyard, a sad end for a life. A forgotten soul lost at sea. It was the vicar's job to search the seashore for bodies and give them a Christian burial

HIRE PURCHASE

Agreement made the _Third_ day of _December_ 193 7

Between Singer Sewing Machine Company, Limited, whose registered office is situate at Singer Building, City Road, London, E.C.1, by _F Martel_ their authorised representative at _7 North Street Quadrant, Brighton_ (herein called "the Owners," which term shall include their successors and Assigns) of the one part, and _J. D. Day._ of _Kiglelere, Willton Road, Eastbourne_ (herein called "the Hirer"), of the other part.   WHEREBY the Owners agree to let to the Hirer the Sewing Machine and/or Property described in the Schedule hereunder (hereinafter called "the Property"), and in consideration thereof

The Hirer agrees :

   a. To pay the Owners on entering into this Agreement the sum of _Twenty Shillings_ (represented by the sum of _Twenty Shillings_ Cash and the allowance made by the Owners for an old machine taken in part exchange from the Hirer) and thenceforth to pay the Owners the sum of _Ten Shillings_ per _month_ payable _monthly_.

   b. To keep the Property in good order and undefaced (damage or loss by fire included), fair wear only excepted, and at all times to allow the Owners' agents and servants, or any other person employed by them, to inspect the same.

   c. To keep the whole of the Property in the Hirer's own custody at his or her address above-mentioned or such other address as the Owners shall approve in writing.   And further not to sell or otherwise deal with the Hirer's interest under this Agreement.

   d. That if the Hirer do not duly perform this Agreement, the Owners may (without prejudice to their right to recover arrears of rent and damages for breach of this Agreement) summarily terminate the hiring and retake possession of the Property ; and for that purpose leave and license is hereby given to the Owners and their agents and servants, or any other person employed by them to enter any premises occupied by the Hirer, or of which the Hirer is tenant, to search for and retake possession of the Property, or any part thereof, without being liable to any suit, action, or other proceeding by the Hirer, or any one claiming under him or her.

   e. That when the hiring is terminated the Hirer shall not on any grounds whatever be entitled to any allowance, credit, return or set off for payments previously made.

   f That any time, indulgence, or concession granted by the Owners to the Hirer shall not affect the Owners' rights or any of them under this Agreement.

   g. That in the event of an old machine being taken in part exchange by the Owners from the Hirer, the same shall forthwith become the property of the Owners, and accordingly no claim shall be made against the Owners under any circumstances for the return of the said old machine.

The Owners agree—

   a. That the Hirer may terminate the hiring by delivering up the Property to the Owners.

   b. That the Hirer may, at any time during the hire, become the purchaser of the Property by payment of the total amount mentioned in the Schedule.

   c. That if such purchase be effected, credit will be given for all payments previously made under this Agreement.

Unless and until a purchase be effected, the Property shall be and continue the sole property of the Owners, and the Hirer shall remain Bailee/Custodier only thereof.

   AS WITNESS the hands of the parties,

The Schedule

Singer Sewing Machine and usual Accessories, Style _15K81, 6-base Elf._ No. _EB-189563_

Cabinet Work _Base, Case, Elf._

Electric Motor No.

Additional Goods

Total Value of the Property Let on Hire is £ _12 : - : -_

Just before Christmas 1937 Joan Boyd (nee Day) as a young Eastbourne girl marched down to the local Singer store and bought a new Singer 15K. The machine cost the princely sum of £12. she paid 20 shillings a month until the machine was hers. Few people know that it was Singer that had the world's first proper hire purchase scheme. Joan is now in her 80's and I still look after her sewing machine.

BLESS YOU

For years now I have called at a closed monastery. I do general repairs on a dozen of their machines.

The first time I called I was taken to an outhouse full of old treadle machines. Several of them were Victorian. Sister Elizabeth asked me to sort out three good ones for the convent and I could do what I liked with the rest. I fixed three beauties using the parts from the other machines and they were moved to the main building. I loaded another three into my car.

I still have them. They are tucked away around the place. I confess to having one of the treadle bases in my garden as a seat. It was the base of a boot-patching machine and is perfect for sitting on. It makes an ideal seat and has worn very well. It could quite easily be put back into working order.

There was just no point in keeping all the rest of the machines and they disposed of them. I know that we would cry now but back then it was not unusual to see sewing machines in skips. In fact that is what started me collecting sewing machines.

Although I had grown up in the sewing-machine trade I had not paid too much attention to old sewing machines. Then, one day on my way home, I passed a skip with six lovely old hand-sewing machines in it. I stopped and, even at that age, I thought it was a terrible shame. No sooner did I get home than I organised a lift back down to the skip. I was too late and they were gone. From that point on I started to save machines from the dump.

The Sister that used one of the convent treadles was very old and going blind. The last time I visited she was 93 and still doing the repairs to their habits. Although she had terrible eyesight once the machine was threaded away she went at the speed of light.

She used to keep a little bit of beeswax next to the sewing machine. This was for two things. Firstly to rub along the seam of anything that stuck to the sewing foot and secondly to wipe over the end of her sewing thread before she tried to thread the needle. She told me it made the thread into a stiff point that she could then jab at the needle until it went through. A great pointer if you have trouble threading a needle.

To see someone that is proficient use a treadle is wonderful. There is a fluid rhythmical motion that is almost mesmerising. She could go as fast as an electric machine, stop in a flash and turn on a sixpence. After each visit, as I leave, she blesses me and adds that she probably won't be seeing me again. I first visited her back in the 1980s and she said exactly the same thing then. Now, all these years later, I am starting to think it is me who is going to bite the dust first!

The last time I called I had to wait. One of the nuns was having the last rites given to her by the priest. We all had to stop work and wait in silence as she passed away. After about forty minutes, as bad as it was, we all started to get impatient. Even the nuns were shuffling around. I had a load of calls to make so I was itching to get going.

Eventually the priest appeared. We waited for the bad news. Then, in a matter of fact soft Irish voice, he said, "She won't be going anywhere today, except maybe to lunch."

At last I could get to the machines and start work! I had eight machines to fix and was well behind my schedule. I ploughed through them in the great hall of the converted manor house.

In the hall hung oil paintings of the nuns in their habits. They all look so dire and sombre. Maybe they did not have much to smile about. Fifty years in any place could take the smile off your face. If you have a sense of humour they are the funniest oil paintings you could ever see.

I was on my sixth machine when I noticed one of the older Nuns making her way towards me from the corner of the room. She was going very slowly, supported by a Zimmer frame. She was making a direct line to me across the oak floor with a determined look on her wrinkled face.

I wondered what she could want. She took ages to get to me. She arrived almost at the same time as my coffee.

Sister Elizabeth, who brought the coffee, said, "You are honoured Alex. Sister Magdalene never comes out of her room and it looks like she is going to pay you a visit."

Sister Elizabeth then tried to talk to her. "How are we today Sister?" Sister Elizabeth asked the old girl, leaning over her in a comforting manner.

"What? What did you say?" She shouts back, loud enough to make the windows rattle.

Elizabeth replied in a much louder voice, "How are we today?"

"Nearly dead, nearly dead!" she answered in a dry creaky whisper.

Sister Elizabeth then handed me my coffee and looked up at the ceiling as if asking for guidance from above, "Your coffee, Alex."

Sister Magdalene on hearing this pipes up, "Coffin? Coffin! What does he want a coffin for? I'm the one that's dying!"

"Not coffin Sister, coffee!" she points out holding up my cup.

"Oh," mutters the old girl, chewing on her gums, deciding if it was worth trying to talk.

"When is your hearing test dear?" asks Sister Elizabeth.

"Two months away. But I'll be dead before that!" she shouts back.

Sister Elizabeth has the patience of a saint but gives up trying to talk to her and leaves the room. By now I am nearly wetting myself with suppressed laughter. It is a comedy sketch straight out of Monty Python. It was so hilarious because it was completely deadpan, no smiles. I tried to calm down as I was in serious danger of rupturing something in my belly as I smothered my laughs.

I was snorting through my nose like a pig in search of truffles.

Sister Magdalene is now standing right next to me, leaning on her Zimmer, looking down at me with a shaky smile across her wrinkled face. She says nothing. Then, to make matters worse, she turns her Zimmer like a car doing a three-point turn and proceeds to shuffle her way back across the room. It was another five minutes before she got to the door and disappeared.

I never did figure out what she wanted. What it was all about? All I knew was that I laughed all the way home to Eastbourne and I still laugh about it now.

She is still there, going strong, with her new hearing aid and all.

A traditional Romany caravan called Border Queen.
The gypsy fortune-teller looks a bit dicey!

THE HAPPY QUILTER

Snap, snap, snap went the Singer,
Clunk, clunk, clunk came the sound.
Mad, mad, mad was the owner,
As she hovered over her machine and frowned.

What, what, what, shall I do,
Scratch, scratch, scratch on her head.
Ring, ring, ring went the phone,
As the Singerman was dragged from his bed.

Please, please, please went the plea,
Huh, huh, huh, came his dozy reply,
Come, come, come around in the morning,
As I need my machine or I'll just die.

Turn, turn, turn went the screwdriver,
Drip, drip, drip dripped the oil.
Sing, sing, sing went the Singer,
As his client came down from the boil.

Sew, sew, sew, sewed the Singer,
Smiles, smiles, smiles all around.
Bye, bye, bye said the Singerman,
As the quilt was sweetly rebound.

Alex. I. Askaroff

The Hastings 'net drying' fishermen's huts are unique and protected buildings.

Canadian geese resting in the Cuckmere Valley before heading north for the winter. The flooding has been good for some animals. I would not have liked to have been a rabbit during the floods!

The old windmill standing just outside of the town of Battle. Windmills were a common sight right up to the 1950's, most are now abandoned to decay, restored or converted to homes like this one.

SEWING MACHINE SERENADE

It had been a good week, all in all. Just the sort I love.

My calls had gone like clockwork, including one to a spirited 95-year-old who still loves sewing and who only gave up driving four years ago. I do not know what she eats but I want some!

One thing she said that killed me was that some ten years ago she had a problem with her old sewing machine. The machine would not stop running on its own. Normally that is usually a simple fault in one of the capacitors for the motor or foot control. She called in our local Singer shop. They told her it was not repairable and sold her a new Singer, taking the old one in part-exchange.

She loved her old Singer, having bought it new in the thirties and she parted with it sadly. While talking to her she was describing it as, "Black and gold, you know the usual type?" Then she said, "Oh yes it was called a Featherweight."

She went on to describe it perfectly, right down to the oil can in the black box.

I was so annoyed. It is just typical of some shops. Cheating her out of a machine that was ten times better than the one they sold her. I did not tell her how popular they are. I thought it would have made it worse. I repaired her new Singer and had it sewing beautifully before I left.

Another call that week really made me smile. It was to a woman whose husband is a great opera singer. He has sung all over the world including at the opening of the Sydney Opera House and he is performing constantly. He had just returned from Russia where he sang a Russian opera. On seeing my name on my work folder he burst into song.

So there I was, in their house fixing their machine and being serenaded with this marvellous and incredibly loud opera. It was one of those moments that you just have to be there to appreciate. Brilliant!

Mind you, I couldn't understand a word of it. Brilliant all the same. It must have rubbed off because I now keep trying to sing *The Volga Boatmen* a song that my dad would often sing to his sons gathered around the fireplace on winters' evenings.

It is always when I am in a rush that I seem to meet the most amazing people. At my last call of the week I bumped into Alan Hope, the joint leader of The Monster Raving Loony Party, one of our most colourful political parties. He had just been to the funeral of his long time friend Screaming Lord Sutch. They put his coffin on the bar of his favourite boozer in Hastings and had a party around him. Then, with a jazz band playing, they marched his coffin through the streets bringing the town to a standstill. What a way to go. Oh yes I did say *joint leader*. The other leader, who makes all the important decisions now, is his cat!

It has been a good week, serenades and all. Tomorrow is another day. A new dawn and new stories waiting to be told. Now, how does that tune go?

Yet another pretty twittern in Pevensey, the perfect place for a stroll. My trials bike is ready and waiting for me to jump on and disappear.

SWIFT AND SURE

In early 1996 I bought a machine from Ron Heat who had retired to St Leonards just along the coast from Eastbourne. Ron was a Londoner born and bred. He grew up in Brixton in the Lambeth area of South London.

During the 1939–45 war he served with the Royal Navy. While he was away on duty a German bomb flattened his home. It was not all bad news as after demob the Government not only trained Ron to become a carpenter but also paid his mum compensation for their bombed house.

When Ron arrived back at his new London home, fresh from his retraining, he found that his mum had saved some of her compensation money for him. She gave him five pounds to buy the necessary tools for his trade. Off Ron marched, down Clapham Road, to a large ironmonger to get all his gear.

In 1946 Colliers, the ironmongers, had been at 134 Clapham Road for nearly a century. They sold everything you could think of in the hardware line. They also sold under their own *Collier* name several types of sewing machines that were made for them over the years.

After a successful trip to Colliers Ron stopped off at the *Prince of Wales* just for a drop of *mother's milk,* as he called it, on his way home. There he met up with a local *Totter* (rag and bone man) called Mr Boe. He had wandered around the Brixton area of London with his horse and cart since Ron was a lad, scratching a living from other people's throw-outs. He had a yard and stables off Cold Harbour Lane.

Boe told Ron he had just the thing for a present for his mum as a thank-you for letting him have the tool money. Boe was a typical wheeler-dealer, always trying to sell something. Boe had a meths iron. A normal smoothing iron that was heated by burning methylated spirits held in a container in the iron. Back in the 1930s and 40s this was quite usual. After a few tipples to celebrate Ron's homecoming they went back to Boe's yard.

At the yard they could not get the meths to light properly. At one stage the iron burst into flames sending Boe's horse racing out of the yard. Both worse for wear after their boozing they chased him up Cold Harbour Lane and found him at the fruit and veg stall on the corner of the road. The stall-owner was trying to pull the great brute away from his carrots and was swearing in good old cockney.

Back at the yard, with the horse secured in the stables, they had a rest. It was then that Ron spotted a sewing machine in the junk. One that had been sold by Colliers some 70 years earlier in 1880. It was an old Colliers *Swift & Sure Lockstitch*. They gave the old machine a good rub with a cloth and found that it was still in fine working order. *Just the thing for his mum* Boe told him. After what Ron described as wheeling and dealing he bought the machine for the 39 shillings he had left.

When Ron got home his mum was delighted with her gift and sewed Ron's first pair of carpenter's overalls on it. She had many years' use out of it before finally leaving it to Ron in her will.

Ron brought it down to St Leonards with him when he retired. He had it buried in the junk in his workshop until he spied my advertisement for Victorian sewing machines. I went along to pick up the machine and spent an enjoyable few hours listening to life in London during the 1940s. After a bit of elbow grease the old Collier Swift and Sure came back to life and it now sits proudly in my display of machines.

If only it could talk! What stories it could tell of life in Victorian London before ending up in Boe's rag and bone yard.

This is a fictitious short story that I had published sometime ago I thought I would pop it into my book. One day I plan to finish his journey.

TEARS OF A CHILD

A troubled dawn threw shafts of uneasy light through the gap in the tatty curtains. I rose slowly to my feet, stretching to ease my aching muscles. I'd had a broken night, sleeping propped against the dormitory door covered by my faithful grey blanket.

My only chance of escape was now. The only window of opportunity was the few short minutes between the door locks releasing and when Fat Bert, with his stale fag and beer breath, made his early rounds.

Although watches were not allowed at the school I had learned to count my heartbeats in time with the main clock in the assembly hall. The clock was perched below a wooden plaque that pronounced to all that entered –

THE WAGES OF SIN ARE PAID BY THE DEVIL

This was supposed to be a reminder of why we were all there. At 15 I had already spent four hard years at the place – four years too long.

I had worked out that around 80 of my heartbeats made 60 seconds and from that I could calculate the three minutes I needed from the first clank of the automatic locks until Fat Bert got to the dormitories. Three minutes were all I needed to make it to the outer fence and freedom.

I knew my route. I had planned it a thousand times as I lay awake night after night at The Bermondsey School for Wayward Boys. We had another name for our secure accommodation that was not so polite.

Lying on an old lumpy horsehair mattress that I shared with several other creatures I had planned my escape repeatedly. Now all my possessions were tied with Jimmy's shoelaces, in a tightly-rolled bundle and tucked under my arm. I could just imagine his face when he went to put his shoes on later, but I knew Jimmy wouldn't mind, he was a mate.

* * * * *

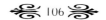 106

Jimmy was a watcher. A boy of few words. When I first arrived at the school he had spent a week watching me from the corners, saying nothing. I was aware of him but, like a new fish in the pond, I spent my days examining my new surroundings. Where I could go and where not.

Jimmy was a complex of emotions. As hard as nails on the outside. Though he was younger than me he was tough. As he walked he swaggered, an instant message to leave him alone. His hands were rough and calloused from endless work. He had a stubby, crooked nose from countless scraps. After a lifetime of borstals his feelings were hidden under a thick skin. Sharp glances from his electric blue eyes told you all you needed to know. Jimmy was nicknamed Sledgehammer because, if he hit you, you did not get up. He was the only boy in the place that the school bully left alone.

Not long after I had arrived I came across Jimmy in the changing rooms. I heard strange noises on my way from the loo and had to investigate. Jimmy was sitting slumped forward on a bench. The summer sun streaming through the haze lighting him as in a beam.

He was sobbing his heart out. I approached him as huge gulps of breath shuddered out of his body. I could not understand what had happened.

"What's up mate," I asked hesitantly.

He slowly opened his hand and there lay the remains of a butterfly. Bits of its delicate wing-scales all over Jimmy's palm.

"I tried to let it out," he gasped through his tears, "but when I went to catch it, I killed it."

Jimmy wanted his own freedom so much that the death of a little creature he had tried to set free was just too much to abide. A lifetime of pain was pouring out of him. We sat in silence, my hand on his shoulder as the only gesture of comfort I knew. From that moment, although we never again talked of the incident, he became my guardian angel. We were mates.

Little did I know that more than twenty years later we would meet again in very different circumstances and it would be Jimmy who would be supporting me. In a million-dollar venture.

* * * * *

Round my neck were my faithful shoes, sent to me two years earlier by my father. A short note inside one said *You may want these, I don't*. It was an unusual offering from a hard and violent man. He probably had no one else to give them to and would not otherwise waste them.

When I first had them they were already worn and several sizes too large. I always took great pride in polishing them with anything from candle wax to pork rind. As time passed my feet pressed at the ends and my big toes had pushed up into two shiny lumps on the brown leather, looking like conkers. I often playfully passed the time pretending to have conker matches clicking my feet together. I did not care. Now they fitted like a glove and were mine – all mine.

A tear-stained letter from Mumsie telling me of the tragic death of my little brother, the brother I had never met, had spurred me into action. Peter had been born, lived and died in less than two years. The letter was short and painful to read. Just the opposite of how happy I was when I had first heard the news that I had a baby brother.

* * * * *

So many times I had dreamed of what we would do together. So many great plans. We were going to rule the world. Now it was all over. Bought to an end by a drunken sod in a fit of rage after drinking away his wages from the pit.

I knew Mum needed me now and I was ready. Ready and willing. I had grown from a scared child cowering in corners to a hard and resourceful fighter. The tears for my brother had turned into hate. Hate for one man. A man to whom I owed my existence but he had never once offered a kind word.

* * * * *

I slipped out of the door and crept silently along the corridor keeping to the side of the polished maple floor. Polished for over a hundred years by thousands of children. A floor polished into a smooth worn surface that sounded like thunder when we all ran for breakfast. Now, as dawn rose, the only sound was the slumber of one hundred and thirty-six forgotten children.

Once at the stairs, I spread my feet wide to reduce any boards creaking, my grey worn socks pushing into the edges of the skirting board as I slowly made my way to the first landing. My socks had been darned many times. It was always a race to get the least mended and the most comfortable pair, after washday Friday. I passed the spot where I got a huge splinter on my first week and thought of matron.

Matron, known as Busty and the butt of most of our gutter humour, was the only nice person in the dump; she had shown me a few welcome moments of tenderness, in a hostile world. The offending item was pulled from my heel. I felt like a wounded lion that had been saved from an agonising fate, I was in love. From then on I would always exchange cheerful smiles when passing her doorway. We all often wondered if she had any kids of her own or if we had become her family. She sometimes wore a sad distant smile, as if she had another life, somewhere in her past.

Once on the landing my next task was to get past the masters' quarters and into the laundry room. The night before I had jammed all the bits of used chewing gum that I could collect into the lock. My favourite place to find old gum was the main sink in the downstairs loo where nearly every time I checked I would find a piece or two stuck to the enamel under the drinking fountain.

I held my breath as I slowly moved the handle down. Everything rested on the door being open.

It opened with a gratifying click. I slithered past the masters' rooms then along the great hall where the silent ghosts of yesterdays teachers stared down disapprovingly from their gilt frames. I got to the laundry shaft where I climbed into the wooden box, pulled the doors closed and untied the rope.

I knew I could get to the ground floor from here because the school bully, Brainless Basher Billy and his gang, had cornered me and he dared me to climb down it. I had to do it. Everyone at the school knew that Basher got huge pleasure from putting kids fingers under the sash windows and smashing them to pulp.

No one ever ratted on him, no one.

On that, my first trip down the laundry chute, I arrived at the washroom

with a thump. I heard Mr Simmonds' call, "Whose there?"

As if anyone would be stupid enough to answer.

As hard as I had pulled the rope, I could not lift my own weight back up, so I had taken a gamble and ran for the main stairs. I had taken them at full speed, three at a time. I was back to my floor before Simmonds had a chance to see me. That dare had given me the escape idea. Little did he know but I had something to thank Brainless Basher Billy for.

This time I slowly slipped down the chute, hand over hand. Down into the dark cold shaft. The only noise the squeaking of the pulley as the rope rolled over it.

Then a nightmare!

My precious bundle that was swung around my back hooked up and caught in the gap between the shaft and the laundry box, jamming it solid. I let go of the rope. Nothing moved. I tried to pull my bundle out but it would not budge. I started to shake and whimper with a nervous cry. All my plans now doomed. I lay slumped in the corner of the laundry box half way down the chute. Visions of the teachers pulling me up and marching me off to the Headmaster rushed through my fraught mind.

Suddenly a feeling came over me. A feeling that I must not, I cannot fail. This was for my brother. I got up, determined to continue.

I made one last desperate attempt to pull the box back up just enough to loosen the bundle. The rope was twisted around my left-hand, snake like, gripping into my flesh. My right hand pulled. Pulled so hard that I felt every muscle in my chest strain.

"Please, God just this once." I whispered, my face contorted, my eyes squeezed tight.

Then, with a jolt it was out. No time to rest. The weight of the box pulled, burning into my arm as it slipped through. Slowly I fought for control and made my way to the bottom.

I dropped, panting. I almost smiled at how my plans to count the magical three minutes with my heartbeat had been blown apart. My heart was

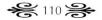

racing like a steam train on the London Express.

I was blowing on my arm to ease the pain when suddenly I became aware that there was a strip of light coming through the crack in the chute doors.

Surely there was no one here at this time of day?

With horror I moved closer to the doors, a shadow passed by and I fell back with a thud. Wide-eyed I froze, holding in a gasp with my hand on my mouth.

Then I slowly moved forward again. Placing one eye up to the crack I could feel the cool air rush past me up the shaft. I started to focus on the large shape. There was Cook. Big fat Cook. He made Fat Bert look positively waif-like. His grubby white apron swinging from his enormous girth as he shuffled about.

I had not counted on this. It had never dawned on me that he would be here this early in the morning.

I watched, a silent onlooker like a rat in a cage, as he threw off his old apron and tried in vain to tie the new one around his belly. He was flapping around like an oversized chicken. He was fighting a losing battle. His fat little fingers stretching uselessly toward his back.

Suddenly he stopped. Then he twisted the apron and tied the knot in front and then slipped the apron around. He walked off with a smirk on his face. Not quite Newton's Theory but a sound discovery nonetheless.

I had a soft spot for Cook. His food was always hot and there was plenty of it as long as you held your nose when he dished up Tuesday's hotpot.

"Get your laughing gear round that," he would chuckle, slopping it into our bowls.

Once Cook had waddled off I made straight for the window. The wonderful smell of fresh washing in the laundry room reminded me how great it was to get those fresh clothes each week. Then past the wicker baskets that used to rattle up and down the school corridors collecting the smelly clothes. I made it to the window and eased it open. Then I slid alligator-like over the sill to the playground below. As I closed the window I heard

footsteps. Bert had started his slow heavy plod up the stairs to unlock the main hall doors and check the dorms. The wood creaking under his weight signalling his progress. I knew his smell would be trailing behind him as it always did.

I tied my shoes on really tight and looked about. All was quiet.

In front of me was the playground and then 300 yards of playing fields. Then the fence – and that beautiful thing beyond – freedom.

Now was the time. I was a good minute behind schedule. A quick look about. I crouched like a hundred-yard dash sprinter, took one last look, then away.

I ran. Ran like a scared rabbit. I bounded across the playground and then the fields. Each stride brought me closer to my goal. I could see the bush where I needed to stop. I could feel my bundle banging against my back urging me on. My feet were digging into the soft soil as I ran.

I was fit. Years of physical training, stodgy food and scrapping makes a child fit. Years of running around the field in endless circles with Mr Gregory the ex-paratrooper at the centre shouting at us like only a gym teacher can.

He would have no slackers. I remembered the day Jimmy fell and cut both his knees. He made Jimmy run around the field another ten times in the rain, blood trickling down his aching legs as the rest of us watched in silence.

I slid to the bush and rolled over. Instantly turning to see if I had been spotted. A single hedge sparrow, startled by my sudden appearance, shot away chattering its annoyance. Otherwise nothing moved, nothing stirred.

My heart was pounding. I gulped down air. I was near the fence. The outside was calling to me. I was so close now I could smell freedom. I moved to the spot in the fence where I had spent the last week digging. I had hidden it with some dead brambles. I moved them and shovelled away the loose earth. My fingernails clawing frantically at the soil.

Then I started pulling at the wire. Within seconds there was almost enough room for me to squeeze under.

On the last day that I had been digging by the fence Jimmy had crept up on me and asked me what I was doing. It was hard to lie to him. He had been my closest mate at the Home and I knew I would never see him again, or so I thought. Even if I was caught and stopped I would be automatically sent to a higher-security establishment.

From bitter experience I had learnt to keep my mouth shut. It was difficult enough trying to get close to the fence without being spotted on our short breaks. When he surprised me I had told him I was burying a blackbird. He helped me mark the spot with a few bits of bramble. Then, typical Jimmy, he insisted on saying a few words over the fake grave including the only part of Who killed Cock Robin that he could remember.

As hard as I tried I could not stop laughing at his rendition. I think I was the only boy in the school who could have got away with laughing at Jimmy.

After some wild digging on my knees I wriggled under the fence, catching my sweater on the twists in the wire. I panicked, as if a teacher was pulling at me trying to stop me. I struggled to get free, ripping the sweater and leaving part of it on the fence.

As I got to my feet I heard a commotion in the distance. I looked back towards the school to see lights being turned on and little figures rushing around behind the windows. There was a second's silence then the still morning air was split with the howling scream of the alarm.

They were too late. Too late to stop me. I was up and running. No money, no way to get home but I was free. I started to run towards the town where I would disappear into the early rush-hour crowd. A needle in a haystack.

I was in my element in the back streets of a town. Growing up a street urchin, as I had done, I could easily blend into the morning scene. Then, over the next few weeks I would make my way home.

As I ran, thoughts came to me of how that evil headmaster, Splinter Harris would never again whack his cane across my palms with that twisted, piercing look of pleasure as I screamed. Never again would I lick my hands and hold them out of the window to catch a breeze to cool the welts.

The terrifying prelude to the pain was watching Harris whack the cane

across his desk to get it just right. Harris was a small skinny man with thin pale lips. He held the school in a grip of terror. The sound of the swish as the cane cut through the air made me run faster. This time I was cutting through the air! I was the swish of the cane with the sound of the wind in my ears, the air rushing into my eyes.

Tears were welling up as I ran, helped a little by the cold morning air, but they were tears of complete joy. The only time I was to ever feel them again was as I held my first child, Peter, who I christened after a little lost soul that I had so longed to meet.

Behind me lay everything I despised and hated. In front of me only dreams. I sprang over old Mabel Baker's flowerbed. I used to watch the wrinkled old girl, through the fence, when she tended to her small patch of garden.

Death had been a patient bystander with Mabel Baker. He had called five times, once for each of her husbands and for two of her seven children but had let her be. At the school there were ghost stories late at night in the dorms of how she had made a pact with the Devil. I envied her so much as she toiled over her little patch of ground, on sunny afternoons, free to come and go as she pleased.

Would she ever wonder, I thought, at the footprints I left in her soil? Where they had come from or how they were paid for in blood?

At last I was free. My feet lifted upon cushions of air as I flew towards the town. This was it! Freedom! The different taste. A flavour that only the caged truly know.

On turning the corner of Blackferry Street I leapt into the air and threw my bundle into the sky announcing to all that I was coming. I shouted, "yes!" to the world and punched the air. My journey from now was still fraught with danger but, as before, I would overcome.

I wiped the tears from my face. I knew that whatever the future held – however many times I was caught, however many times they would try to break my spirit – this was the first escape! The one that I would always remember. The one that would always mean the most to me.

This was my greatest escape and the beginning of my hardest journey.

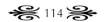 114

RESTLESS SLUMBER

The dark of the night seems to whisper a lie,
But with the morning light it passes by.
I awake to see the night take flight,
And watch the crimson sky alight.

The cold wind that bent the giant yew has fled,
Fled north in search of Valhalla and bed.
Whilst all around in quiet slumber lay,
I am up to witness the start of day.

Awoken from a turbulent, troubled sleep,
I have an appointment with dawn to keep.
I hear the first bird of morning sing,
And sense the comfort that it does bring.

The tormenting day that lays ahead,
Is for a moment lost, all worries shed.
As Sun and Moon chase across our Earth,
I witness the daybreak, another rebirth.

Simple things that help unclutter the mind,
Are so elusive and hard to find.
Now I treasure this moment, so terribly rare,
And soak up the dawn without a care.

A.I.Askaroff
Daybreak

LOUISA'S STORY

Louisa Janes is another Londoner born in the great city just south of the River Thames and within earshot of Bow Bells. There is an old saying that if you are born within half a mile of Bow Bells or can hear their chimes then you can call yourself a *Cockney*. This was certainly true in Louisa's case. "Always remember you are a Cockney," her mum used to say to her as a child, "and be proud of it girl."

Growing up in London during the 1920s was full of excitement for a young girl. These were little things like picking up her parents' fruit and veg from Covent Garden or running along the Embankment after school. She used to chase the ravens that wandered down from the Tower for scraps of food.

They now clip the ravens' wings to stop them flying as an old saying tells that if all the ravens leave the Tower the Royal Family shall come to an end.

When Louisa was 12 her mother, Eva, bought a brand new Singer Model 66. Eva was so eager to get the machine home that she could not wait for the delivery cart that would normally take the machine to her home. Between Louisa and Eva they managed to push the Singer treadle along the bumpy streets almost a mile from the shop to her home. As they got to her street, several of their neighbours came out to watch.

One neighbour, who Louisa always disliked, shouted out to her mother, "I see your little scallywag is being useful for a change." As the machine went into the house they all started to clap.

Because of the high cost of the new machine she bought it on the never-never. A common way to purchase a sewing machine when they could cost a month's wages. Eva would make the weekly payments of half-a-crown to the Singer shop. Eva did a deal with her daughter about the repayments. If Louisa took the money to the Singer shop every Friday afternoon then Eva would teach her how to sew.

Thereafter, every week for what seemed like years, Louisa took the payment down to the Singer dealer and bought the week's groceries on the way home. In turn, as promised, that evening she would have her weekly sewing lesson.

It all paid off big time in the 1930s when, as a young woman, she left school. She managed to get a job straightaway at a firm called Laura Lees. She passed her sewing tests with ease. Laura Lees was a big fashion house producing beautiful evening gowns and dresses.

Unlike today, where most factories have sewing lines, or production circles, that produce parts of a garment piece by piece, they would make a complete garment in one go. This had its ups and downs. The individual was responsible for her own quality control. If there was a mistake there was no one else to blame. On the other hand each saw the final product as all her own work and could be proud of it. Louisa worked at Laura Lees for four years up until the outbreak of World War Two.

By 1940 she found herself on a bus filled with strangers heading for the North and the industrial heartland. She was being sent to a factory to help with the war effort. "Always remember you are a Cockney and be proud of it my girl," were the last words her mum spoke as she mounted the bus.

She ended up in Birmingham putting together oil pumps for Spitfire engines. "Quality, quality, quality," the line manager would preach, "One mistake will cost the lives of our brave pilots."

On and on, every day, quality was preached to them. Louisa had the good training at Laura Lees to fall back on for, although the products were very different, the need for getting the quality just right was the same.

Back in London after the war, the docks had been badly damaged by German bombing raids. The factory where she worked had been destroyed. It was rebuilt and later changed names to Eastex but Louisa never returned to work there. Instead she managed to get a job that she loved in an office. No more piecework for her.

Louisa was paid a flat hourly rate for working and, as soon as the boss was out of sight, the usual office gossip started. Who was seeing whom and what show was worth going to and so on.

The only sewing Louisa did now was for her own pleasure. Eventually she

inherited her mum's Singer 66 treadle. Louisa still sews on it to this day. I was called to service it for the very first time after over 60 years of faithful service. Some new machines today have trouble getting out of their guarantee period. Lucky for me or I would be out of work!

The Singer needed some attention, nothing life-threatening and easily fixed. Louisa told me that the Singer was the only item that she still had from her mother.

She often sits and stares at the machine, thinking of mother and her trips down to the Singer shop every Friday with a half-crown. She can still hear her mother saying, "Wherever you end up in the world, my girl, never forget the sound of Bow Bells and always be proud of your roots. Hold your head high and never forget you are a Cockney my girl. Never forget you are a Cockney."

The Pavilion tea rooms along Eastbourne seafront. Simply a lovely place for afternoon tea, especially when the pianist is in.

SOPPY SUZY

I have a customer that brings her Bernina Minimatic down from Blackpool to have me service it each year. She visits her relatives here while I sort out the machine. The last time I saw it I noticed that the bearings were bone dry and there were blue heat-marks around them. I asked what had happened. This is what she told me.

She had been sewing an evening gown in her sewing room all afternoon. She was wearing it to a function that night. She finished up and changed into her new frock. Off she and her husband went, wrapped up warm against the cold winter air.

On arriving back home a few hours later, they heard a strange noise coming from the sewing room upstairs. They crept up to the room and slowly opened the door. Prepared for intruders, her husband was armed with his umbrella, one just cannot get decent weapons over here you know since they banned guns!

As the door creaked ajar they saw the Bernina on the sewing cabinet running full pelt. Beneath the table their dozy dog, Suzy, was asleep with her head resting on the machine's foot control.

Suzy is a Great Dane and when she heard them enter the room she casually lifted her head. The sewing machine ground to a halt, almost with a sigh of relief. A haze of smoke lifted from the machine and hung over it like a mushroom cloud. It was the last of the oil burning off!

Apparently Suzy had slunk into the sewing room and, feeling the foot control still warm from the earlier use, decided to rest her head upon it. Now Suzy is a lazy dog by any measure. So lazy in fact that she even had the tape measure and a pair of snips lying on her that had vibrated off the table. She had remained there too bone-idle to even shake them off. They guess the machine could have been running flat-out for as long as four hours!

The machine, amazingly, had almost no damage and after a good service ran perfectly. Soppy Suzy as they have now christened her has been banned from the sewing room. I wonder how many new machines could stand that sort of hammering? Very few that's for sure.

In spring when the first green flash of new grass shoots up, the Downs look like a duvet thrown across a bed.

Many parts of East Sussex are still heavily forested. Wild boar have been spotted roaming the woods.

An Urban Myth comes to Life

Terminus Road, the main street in Eastbourne, is a long road leading through the centre of the town. It ends at the beautiful and famous Carpet Gardens on the seafront. They lead on to the best Victorian pier in England.

The pier stretches out into the English Channel and it is full of small shops selling sweets and candyfloss, doughnuts and silly little seaside toys. You can fish off the end of the pier for lovely cod or have your palm read by Madame Clarissa. The pier is one of the quintessential British seaside necessities.

For many years, in Terminus Road, there was a Singer shop. Before World War II in the heyday of the Singer company when, as their advertisements read *The only machine worth having is a Singer,* the shop did a roaring trade servicing the surrounding areas. In fact business was so good that Eastbourne supported two Singer shops. Mr and Mrs Norman ran the other, down Seaside Road less than a mile distant.

The Chapmans later ran the Seaside shop with their mechanic Peter Ruffle busily repairing machines in the shop's basement. A Mrs Taylor would do all the demonstrations of the wonderful new models in the shop.

Our story is about Albert Putter. Albert was just 14 when he left school and was sent off to work at the Terminus Road Singer shop. That was in the summer of 1939. His duties were to include sweeping the shop floor, making the tea and, once trained, the collection and delivery of the sewing machines on the shop's trusty bicycle.

The bicycle had been specially converted to carry the heavy sewing machines. Some of his trips would take him way into the countryside to market towns such as Hailsham and Heathfield. It was not uncommon for Albert to make a 25-mile round trip on his bike loaded with sewing machines. Can you imagine just how hard that must have been!

In the 1930s electricity was becoming popular. Sewing machines were being fitted with motors and lights. Many machines were converted from hand to electric. The conversion was all done for the princely sum of £5.00.

This does not seem much today but it was more than two weeks wages in pre-war days.

It became one of Albert's jobs to fit the motor conversions. Fitting motors was the beginning of the end for hand machines. Until then only treadle machines had allowed you to sew with both hands free and when you became good with the treadle, as I have said before, you could turn on a sixpence.

Before electricity and without a treadle the only way you could sew was with one hand or you could find a willing partner who would turn the handle while you sewed. I have met many a woman who, as a child, turned granny's sewing-machine handle for her.

One of the stories that I had always heard since childhood and that had circulated for many years was about the deliberate destruction of old sewing machines by the Singer shops. This was said to be to stop them being used for resale and, consequently, the loss of a new machine sale.

It was one of those urban myths. I had always been sceptical of it. The idea seemed so diabolical to me, the destruction of those wonderful old machines. Well, all that was about to change when I met Albert Putter.

The destruction of sewing machines was one of his jobs.

I met Albert after his wife had called me out to look at her old machine that had seized up from lack of use. Over a cup of tea Albert told me how he used to take great pleasure in his monthly ritual with the sledgehammer. It was not the ham-fisted affair that one might think but a well-orchestrated event.

The machines to be destroyed were collected at the shop. They were usually machines that had been part-exchanged. They included Singers but mostly the older mother-of-pearl inlaid Victorian machines. There were old Vestas and the like. Machines that collectors would probably kill for today!

A chap called Mr Mane would come down from London with his book of records at the end of each month. It was his job to make a list of all the different types of machines and the serial numbers of those to be destroyed. Once Mane had listed the machines and their serial numbers they were taken out to the back yard. In the yard Albert would set about them with a sledgehammer and smash them to pieces.

This destruction was carefully overseen by Mane until he was satisfied that each machine and all its parts were destroyed. Then he would close his book, bid farewell to Albert and proceed to the next establishment.

I would love to know what they did with the records they kept. It would prove fascinating reading. There must have been many books with endless lists of machines that had bitten the dust under a Singer-supervised hammer. It would, at least, let us make a bit of sense of the odd numbers of the old machines that turn up today.

If this practice was worldwide, and had been going on for many decades, imagine how many thousands of machines would have been destroyed this way. I have been told that many years later some of the bigger shops were set up with huge seven-ton presses that simply crushed the machines. Talk about removing the competition!

However the story does not finish there. On the yard floor was a valuable resource, scrap iron. As soon as Mr Mane was gone Albert was sent off to fetch the local Rag-'n'-Bone man, a totter called Amos Burley who scoured the streets of Eastbourne for anything that he could sell-on or recycle.

Amos would arrive on top of his cart pulled by Thunder a huge carthorse that had spent the first 15 years of his life pulling beer barrel drays for the Star Brewery in Old Town.

Amos would calculate, with a lifetime's experience, the rough weight of the scrap machines. A bit of haggling would ensue and cash would change hands. Then Albert would load the cart and off Thunder would plod, his bells ringing to let all and sundry know that the Rag-'n'-Bone man was around.

I remember well the great horses that pulled the drays and the draymen. Hard, tough men that spent their days loading and unloading beer barrels. Every day on the way to school I used to walk past the Star Brewery. Sometimes, when the coast was clear, I would slip through the yard that cut between Star Road and Ocklynge Road. I would peer into the steaming rooms where the brewers were busy at their timeless art. More than once I was chased off with some colourful words and a hobnailed-boot up the backside.

Although it has long since been demolished, to make way for another block of homes, I can smell that brewery now. The Sussex hops, so rich and pungent, the malt and barley that made those wonderful local beers so special. On calm days you could cut that smell with a knife. On windy days you could close your eyes miles away and walk to the brewery just using your nose.

A few times a year the brewery horses, that in my time were kept for show more than any real work, were tarted up for local events. What a sight they seemed to me, a young schoolboy on my way to St Mary's School. Those great beasts resplendent in polished harness with silver and brass metalwork and tinkling bells were a magnificent sight. They stood around 17 hands and were strung from head-to-foot with ornamental brasses that caught the morning light as they were led, clip-clopping, up the street from their stables near Motcombe Park to the brewery.

Amos Burley had premises in Leslie Street just off Seaside. From his yard he would send the old iron to a scrap yard at the port of Newhaven some 12 miles along the coast. From that yard it was shipped back to a foundry to be used to help refine molten pig iron into good steel to start the whole process once more.

I wonder how many sewing machines are lampposts and drain covers all over England today? During the war years, when raw materials were in very short supply, sewing machines along with any other sort of metal, even the railings outside your house, were taken away and sent to help make more steel for the war effort.

Things went on in that same manner – with Albert smashing machines one day and delivering new machines on his trusty bike the next.

Then, one sunny morning, a German bomber took a fancy to drop its payload on Eastbourne instead of London. Eastbourne was the most bombed town in the South East during the war. Not because of its industry but because it happened to be on a flight path to our great city. Eastbourne was the first and last chance they had to drop bombs on English soil.

My wife's grandfather, Cyril, was sitting in his bungalow when the bombs hit during one of these raids. It shattered every pane of glass in the rows of council greenhouses in Kings Drive where he was foreman. He, like his brother before him and his father before that, had looked after Eastbourne's city nurseries since Victorian times. Cyril had been responsible, for decades, for the beautiful flowers that made our town the envy of others across the land.

The explosion lifted his bungalow and dropped it back down, crooked by one inch from its original foundations. It stood crooked to the day it was demolished 60 years later. Albert and the Singer shop-assistant survived the attack by hiding under a large heavy cutting table. Alas, the shop suffered severe damage and the shop was never reopened. Albert's job had come to a swift and violent end.

Years later another Singer shop opened further up in the next street but things were never the same.

After the war, as you can imagine, for nearly a decade there was a huge shortage of raw materials. Consequently sewing machines were scarce. Sewing machine shops had terrible trouble getting machines and supplies. This is when the major boom in reconditioning started. Rather than be destroyed, a machine was completely taken apart and the frame sent back to the factory for re-japanning or enamelling. Later it would be reassembled to produce a nearly new machine.

They survive today in 1950s Beechwood cases with modern gold transfers. I often come across them and it is usually quite a shock for the owner to find that her machine is late Victorian.

It was the end of an era. No more Amos Burley with his horse and cart bargaining for scrap. No more the clink of shattered castings on the yard floor at the back of the Singer shop and no Mr Mane with his book of numbers.

It is an era passed into history. Gone and almost forgotten now. Albert Putter and his wife still reside in a sleepy village near our seaside resort. They remember those early days with great affection.

A branch of Yana's family ran *Medway Sewing Machines* in Maidstone. As a young man, learning the trade from his father, Uncle Gordon spent many an hour carrying out the laborious reconditioning tasks. Such was the scarcity of new machines that this was the only option to keep the trade going.

When a customer wanted to buy a new sewing machine it was the normal procedure to be put on a long waiting list and, when the next machine arrived, you would be contacted. I have met people that have waited over a year for their new machine. What a difference today now there is a glut of new *plastic pigs* chasing ever-fewer customers.

There was an old joke that Singer shops used to have during the late 1940s and 50s – I love it.

A woman would arrive at the local Singer shop to buy a new sewing machine. "I would like to purchase a new Singer," she would announce.

The proprietor would look at her in dismay and reply, "Wouldn't we all madam. Wouldn't we all!"

Me and my trusty Land Rover with the Sussex Downs fading away in the disance. Some days when the sky is blue and the hills are green, going to work is a pleasure.

DAY TRIP

Some days, when we have a build-up of machines to deliver back to our customers and I am going to a nice part of the County, Yana comes with me. It is her chance to escape the phone and the daily pressures of our sewing-machine business.

We set out before dawn with a car full of sewing machines and headed towards Hastings. Our first drop woke the family. That was quite lucky because, as I walked into the house, a waft of gas hit me. They were unaware of the smell or that their boiler was leaking fumes. I left them with their Elna SU and a reminder to get their boiler sorted.

Next call, to the woman's grandmother, was to drop off a 1920s Frister & Rossmann with lovely Egyptian scrollwork transfers. Kids often play with sewing machines, they are a main source of my income, the little darlings! 30 years before this Frister & Rossmann had been taken apart and it had not been used since.

I come across so many customers that have their grandmother's machines. It seems to follow a pattern. If your mother sews you are not inclined to sew yourself. Of course this is not always the case but it is quite common. Grandmothers seem to have more time and grandchildren more interested in learning. That is probably because of those trips that children do to *granny's* and sewing was something that she could teach to a child and so share a common interest.

Thus, sewing often jumps a generation. If the grandmother catches a child of eight or nine she can pass on a love of sewing that lasts a lifetime.

After the Frister, I dropped off an Italian Necchi Mirella. These are one of my favourite machines. OK, so I have loads of favourites! What makes the Necchi so great is the quality of the engineering in the machine. I always look on Necchi as the Ferrari of the sewing world.

That was before they went all plastic on me.

It also has a super little device to cope with power cuts. On the side of the machine is a small handle. When you have no power just insert the handle, disengage the motor and away you go.

Then we went on to drop off a 1910 Singer 66 that had needed a lot of hard work to get it sewing again. The owner had bought it from a market for a fiver and then called me in to repair it. I left with her praising my work and a bless you. Mind you, her husband is a wine specialist. I could not help thinking I should have fixed something of his, like his car, and come away with a few bottles of Champagne!

By now we had arrived at one of the most wonderful towns in the country and a personal favourite of mine – Battle.

The weather was a typical autumn day. Storms brewing in the Atlantic were sweeping across our island. As we arrived in Battle people were hurrying for shelter, their heads bowed against the wind. We parked near Battle Abbey and walked up to the Pilgrims Rest. This beautiful medieval building has remained much the same for centuries. It is a place where the weary traveller would rest for the night.

Mind you, we only wanted breakfast!

Moving in to sit beside an open fire we woke Sally, a Bulldog, and she gave us a nonchalant sniff before resuming her job of soaking up the warmth spilling from the crackling fire. Before long I too was warming up. One side of me roasting from the fire but the other still cold from draughty windows.

As I looked out of the diamond-shaped leaded-glass windows, slightly obscured by dried flowers and lavender, I saw school children walking through the huge gates of the Abbey to the school in its grounds. They were squealing with joy as the gusts of wind raced past them through the archway of the Abbey.

Claire served our breakfast in front of the fire. She looked as if she had come out of a different time. Perhaps she had? Her family have their roots in Battle as far back as anyone can remember.

I could just imagine her with jugs of ale pushing past merry revellers at The Pilgrim's Rest. All laughing and singing in the atmosphere of a forgotten age. The roaring fire dancing on the faces of many strangers. Perhaps they were on a pilgrimage or maybe just market traders off to the many towns with their goods. All staying together for the night, friends for a few short hours then strangers once again.

Breakfast was the traditional English *fry up* – bacon, eggs, fried bread, beans, sausages as big as the plate, mushrooms simmered in butter, fried tomatoes and a mug of piping hot tea. Not the sort of breakfast for a calorie counter!

Sally suddenly showed an interest in us and rested her huge head on Yana's leg looking, no, pleading for food. The fact that she had no waistline – the dog, not Yana – proves that this tactic works well. Soon she was feasting on fried bread with us. Her owner was not amused by her gentle and persuasive methods. He light-heartedly told her off, calling her *fidgety britches,* local slang for someone who irritates you. Sally dropped her head and sulked off to resume her duty by the fireplace.

From any position The Pilgrims Rest is so picturesque that you can sit for ages and just stare. The low old ceiling in one room is supported by huge oak beams blackened from centuries of open fires. There is not a straight wall in the place. They are made of lath and lime plaster. Plaster being a more pleasant description of the material that was made with horse manure among other things.

I was quite happy nibbling on marmalade toast when the mottled oak entrance door was heaved open. In came another customer followed by a blast of wind and a handful of autumn leaves. The leaves rushed in and, for a brief second, they were full of life like a mass of travellers running for the last train. Then, as the door closed, in another second, they fell to the floor motionless.

I watched to see if a leaf would make a break for the door and a second chance to dance down the street but all lay still. My trance was broken, we paid for our meal and carried on our way.

We wiggled our way back down country lanes past Ashburnham Place that is now a Christian conference centre. It was once a large country manor where the lords and ladies hunted wild boar and stag. Funnily, just to

129

remind us of those days, we passed a few pheasants clawing the grass verge for seeds.

Our corner of England still has deer and wild boar roaming the forests, though I have never seen the latter. Claims of their attacks on sheep are common gossip, over frothy hop-rich beer, in local pubs. I met a man who once had a team of Husky dogs that he used to run through the forests of East Sussex. He came face to face with a wild boar one stormy night.

Ted had called me out to repair a Singer model 15k that he used to make the dog-leads and harnesses for the team. He told me of the time he was racing through the woods one evening. It was getting dark and the team was pulling hard down a forest track. Suddenly the lead dog collapsed. The harness had managed to wrap itself around the dog's throat and in the dark he had not noticed.

He quickly unhooked the dog and rubbed his chest but it was no good, the dog had given his last breath pulling his master. Distraught, Ted sat by his dog and wept. His partner, whom he was racing, caught up with him and saw what had happened. He picked up the Husky by its four legs and slammed it down onto the ground, then repeated it a second time. The dog suddenly came back to life, sat up and started to lick Ted all over his face. Ted just broke down and cried some more. Ted was an ex-army man so it took a lot to make him break.

During the whole episode they were being watched.

As darkness stole across the forest they became aware of something in the woods that had been quietly observing the whole affair. A huge boar then moved from his hiding position onto the path in front of them. This was the first time either of them had ever seen such an animal. Ted estimated it must have been between 600 and 800 lbs (290–380 kg).

The boar made no threatening moves but its very presence in the failing light of the forest was enough. He was letting them know who was boss. He stared at them with his bristles up and he snorted. The dogs started to howl in fear. Ted and his mate made a hasty retreat. They have never ventured into that forest at night since.

On our way home we dropped off one more machine. A plastic cheapie known in the trade as a *plastic pig*. About as useful to the serious sewer as a one-legged dog to a shepherd.

Then, with all our work finished for the morning and our bellies full I pointed the Land Rover south, towards the downs and headed for home.

THE COMMON ORCHID ON THE DOWNS

The Downs ooze a wealth of flora including many orchids. Except for the bleakest time of year the Downs are always full of interest. There are 51 different orchids growing wild in Britain. Orchids are said to be the sexiest flowers on earth and in Victorian England possession by females of orchids was banned. Old folklore tells that orchids grew where animals had mated! There is a £5,000 fine for digging them up so if you do find one just admire it.

WATCH OUT *GROCKLES* ABOUT

As word of my work spread, business became hectic. Sometimes it would get so busy that I felt like jumping off Beachy Head to disappear into the murky depths of the English Channel leaving a note at the top of the cliffs saying, *One sewing machine repair too many.*

Just so that I do not have to answer the phone to a woman like the one that I had just spoken to.

"I have just bought a bulb for my machine. Why won't it work?"

I listen with growing unease, "Is it the right bulb for your machine?" I asked in a vain hope of trying to help a complete stranger.

"How would I know?" replies the women.

"How would I know either?" I reply.

The situation is hopeless I have a person I have never met giving me abuse down the line over a bulb that she bought from a food store!

Then there was the customer that phoned to complain about another sewing machine repairman. What can I do? I have to listen to a tirade of abuse about someone I have never seen, from a person who appears to me to be completely mad.

Or my worst yet. A customer phoned from Uckfield. "My needle-bar clamp will not tighten on my new machine. I only bought it from you last month! I am very disappointed!"

Even after talking to her for ages she did not calm down. It was seven o'clock in the evening. I agreed to go straight away to sort it out. It took ages to get there, arriving to more abuse. When I got to the machine, sure enough the needle-bar clamp would not tighten up.

"Well, it will not tighten up without a needle in it." I said to her. "You need a needle in the machine for the clamp to tighten onto."

The woman looked at me down her nose as if I was stupid. "Look, look! It is all loose and wobbly."

"Yes, but if you put a needle in, it tightens up perfectly. Just as it is designed to do."

"Well it is not good enough!" she spouts, her husband standing behind her in support.

I'm left without words. What can I say to the woman? I ask her, "How much sewing do you do on the sewing machine with no needle in?"

To this question there was a sudden realisation that she was just stupid. But, rather than apologise, she started saying that it should be made clear in the instruction book. I am shuffled out of the house like a bag of rubbish with a 20-mile trip to get home.

Some days you just cannot win.

The sewing machine business became even more hectic after the closure of our local Singer shop. After 70 years of trading, Singer in Eastbourne finally closed its doors. It was sad that this happened but not unexpected.

Eastbourne was in full-tourist-swing for the summer. Coach-loads arriving daily to the hundreds of hotels that line our promenade.

The tourists are easy to spot. They come down to the seaside in their normal clothes then hire one of the council deck chairs for the day. They guard them with their lives. It would be easier to get any one's wife from him than the deck chair.

Then they roll their trousers up to just below the knee and roll their Woolworth's polyester shirtsleeves up to the elbows. No attempt is made to remove their socks or shoes. They plonk themselves down onto the chairs and sit, like King Canute by the sea trying to stop the tide from coming in. About every half-hour they pick up their chairs and march up the beach a bit as the tide moves in.

This goes on along the entire stretch of the seafront. I would love to see it all in slow motion on a video.

Oh, I forgot, the most important essential piece of equipment they all seem to carry is a handkerchief. They spend a good twenty minutes tying knots into each corner of it before placing it on their heads. A proud symbol of their northern tribe. Then they sit on the seafront all day until they are lobster-red. Suntan lotion is considered for posh lily-white-skinned folk only.

Locals refer to them as *Grockles* and I love them dearly. Eastbourne would never be the same without them. We are a tourist town, without these people it would be deserted like it is most of the winter months. We get around 2.5 million tourists a year. I talk about our visitors in the friendliest terms of affection. I have never met people on holiday here that do not have a good time.

As I cycled the four-mile length of the Eastbourne promenade with Yana, we saw the whole town come to life. Most of our visitors are mature and do nothing in a rush. The only thing you hear after 9 pm is the rattle of false teeth and the odd wheelchair squeaking down the road!

I exaggerate but you get the idea.

We cycled along as the holidaymakers were oozing out of the seafront hotels, like a jar of spilt honey, with absolutely no hurry or haste, slowly flowing onto the beaches. By the time we returned from our ride the beaches were heaving with the summer bustle of holiday life.

The French market was taking place in the town centre as it does most years. Traders from France pack their goods into vans and head for the channel ports to come to coastal cities like Eastbourne. They line their goods up for sale along the pedestrian precinct in the town centre.

Everything that you can imagine about French food is here. The smells are heavenly. Croissants. Lovely French-stick bread baked the night before. Cheeses of all descriptions. Only the French can really make a great cheese – or so they tell me. Brie, Camembert, Roquefort, Samos garlic cheese, all exuding an aroma to die for.

Next the cake stall where they are cooking fresh pancakes to order and tiny sugar-covered doughnuts. Then the onion stall, not just one type of onion mind you but twenty. Small ones, large ones, red and white, shallots, pickling onions and garlic, even smoked garlic.

The stalls stretch the entire length of the precinct with fresh fruit, sweets, jams and wines. The whole street takes you to a mini-France. The traders create a charming atmosphere as they chat in French while drinking strong coffee.

Then, at the end of the day, it all disappears as suddenly as it arrived. Tomorrow they will be home in France. A country that is only a stone's throw across the water but a million miles away in culture and tastes.

Walking along the stalls brought back my extended stay in France many years ago. All the French produce made me so hungry that we bought a chicken and had it with a bottle of soft fruity red wine from the French Muriel vineyards.

Back at work I had a nice and totally unexpected surprise. I had called on a customer who lives not ten miles from me. While I was fixing her temperamental Singer *Touch-n-Throw* 760, I noticed an oil painting on the wall that looked very familiar. I could not put my finger on who was staring back at me but I knew the face from somewhere.

When I asked who it was the woman told me the most amazing thing. No, not *What a handsome devil you are!* but she said that she was married to the grandson of James Galloway Weir. This stopped me in my tracks. Surely there was some mistake? There was no mistake. I was in the house of Weir's grandson. The oil painting was of the man himself.

JG Weir imported the famous Charles Raymond machines from Canada during the latter half of the 19th century before deciding to chuck it all in and become a politician. He claimed to have invented his small 55-shilling sewing machine. Before the Trade Descriptions Act 1890 he could legally mark machines any way he wished.

I was fascinated by my customer's descriptions, that had been passed down through the family, of the great man. For instance when James Weir was trying to make his fortune money was tight. He was on the verge of patenting the thread tensioning device for the top of his machine and had spent all his money on patent attorneys. He had to sell his house and he slept beneath the bench of his workshop in Glasgow.

He came from a huge family. He was one of fifteen children, several of whom died. Apparently it was watching his mother sew all day that made him realise the potential of a cheap sewing machine. It was a slow road to making his fortune and a very different story from the one that I was familiar with in the *history* books.

His generosity after becoming wealthy took me by surprise. He would often take beggars off the streets and feed them at his table in his large London residence. Apparently he never trusted banks and had money stashed away in false books in his library.

When you find out the real side of a person, not the one that the public normally sees, it is so fascinating. History judges him quite harshly now, but he appeared to be a much nicer man than we ever knew. It was a marvellous chance-meeting and one that I will never forget.

Dawn breaking over Eastbourne seafront

EASTBOURNE

Oh Eastbourne, Eastbourne by the sea,
Dressed up in all her finery.
Beautiful gardens, such a show,
A thousand places to see and go.

Guesthouse frying pans sizzle away,
Starting another fun filled day.
Buckets and spades deckchairs too,
Red noses glow under skies of blue.

Famous people have also come,
To see the sights, soak up the sun.
They take the air refresh the soul
Arrive in parts, but go back whole.

A diamond in a blanket of green,
The sand, the sea, the perfect scene
The jewel of our coasts, shinning bright,
Oh Eastbourne, Eastbourne what a sight.

ALEX. I. ASKAROFF

DUEL AT DAWN

Around my area of East Sussex, picturesque villages are dotted like fallen stars on the green blanket that rolls off the fabulous South Downs. Near Lewes our county town there are perfect little villages such as Firle, Glynde, Ringmer, Ripe, Laughton and many more.

Near Ringmer lie two grass-covered mounds of earth side by side. According to local folklore they are the unmarked graves of two soldiers that died for love. They lie beside Norlington Lane that meanders lazily through the breathtaking countryside around the foot of my beloved South Downs.

I had heard the soldiers' story many years before from a sprightly 90-year-old who was born and bred in Lewes just up the road from Ringmer. However I had never paid it much attention until I came across their graves.

What a priceless June day it was! Cotton-wool clouds drifted across a perfect-blue sky. Crops were shimmering in late morning sunlight as I drove past forgotten footpaths that wound along the edges of ripening cornfields. The Downs, not yet turned brown by the summer heat, were exuding a vibrant green that I am sure only exists in our corner of the world.

Swallows darted and dived on the blustery warm thermals that still held a hint of spring. Fields of blue flax rippled like landlocked seas where no ship would ever sail.

Yes, it was a perfect day!

I was on my usual travels around the county repairing one machine after another. I travelled down a back road from Ringmer into Norlington Lane and had overshot a customer's house. As I turned in a small lay-by, I came face to face with the two mounds by the roadside. The council had just mown the grass. It was a poignant and unexpected moment as history suddenly came to life.

Our tale goes back to the 18th century. Smuggling was rife along the coast. Infamous gangs crept silently through the moonlit countryside with their booty. To curb the influx of wines, spirits and tobacco, strict new laws are passed. James Watt is trying to perfect the steam engine to help kick-start the industrial revolution while George III was fighting two battles, one against madness, the other against American colonists who wanted to rule themselves.

New laws were passed to clamp down on general country felonies. The poaching act of 1770 carried an automatic six-month prison sentence. If you were caught a second time you faced a public whipping with the benefit of a whole year at his Majesty's pleasure. Duelling was outlawed, punishable by execution. Regardless, in Norlington Lane two soldiers lay dead, soaked in their own blood.

It all seems to have started when a beautiful lass from Ringmer began making eyes at two soldiers that were billeted nearby. The men were regimental service colleagues and friends. As with many tragedies, both had met and fallen head-over-heels in love with her.

With the realisation of the love-triangle their friendship turned to hate and a wedge was driven between them. The scene was set for a deadly drama. One cold misty morning, some two hundred and thirty years ago, down a small country lane these former friends faced each other.

It is unclear with the passing of time whether the crack of pistols echoed around the hillside or if their fate was sealed by the clash of swords. Whatever the weapons, the outcome was the same, both were fatally wounded and died where they had fought. It must have been a tragic scene, two friends fighting alone. Gentlemen in despair blinded by love and rage. Both meeting an untimely end.

A Shakespearean tragedy played out in a little lane with the backdrop of the downs. Far from the romantic idea we have of those times. If either had survived he may well have hung for the crime of duelling.

As a form of posthumous punishment the army refused to collect or bury the dead soldiers. Local farmers dug their graves where they fell and made simple wreaths for them. A plaque now marks the spot where two friends lie side by side for eternity.

In life their love for one woman had torn them apart with tragic consequences. Perhaps in death they are once again united?

Folklore has it that, even now, on a still autumn night when the harvest moon hangs low in a star-studded heaven the haunting cries of a young woman float across the countryside and the next day, fresh flowers will be found on the men's graves.

The Council nurseries in the 1960's full of geraniums for the seafront carpet gardens. The heat and the smell was something my wife will always remember. Iris Cottington is checking up on her husband's work.

BIRTHDAY SURPRISE

Mary Wilding arrived into the world in the early 1920s in London. She shared her terraced house, south of the River Thames, with her brother and their Mum and Dad. Her father had fought in the Great War and was sent home with a piece of shrapnel that had been pulled out of his body as a souvenir.

The early years through the 20s and 30s were hard times for them. Her parents had married under-age and, consequently, they were refused a married person's allowance. Because of that her dad worked all the hours he could on London Transport. By 1940 a strange metal-roofed contraption called an Anderson shelter was an addition to their back garden.

Daily bombing raids were the reply to Chamberlain's *Peace in our time.*

During one terrible night in early 1941 the bombing was so severe they did not dare run for the shelter but crouched in a doorframe. London was being hit by the Blitz.

A bomb exploded in the street outside their house throwing Mary straight out of the house and bouncing her off the Anderson shelter where she was supposed to be. The family survived but the house and contents were completely gutted by fire.

For the duration of the war there was a huge community spirit where everyone helped each other.

During this period if you needed help you would go to the local council depot. At the depot all the furniture and possessions that could be saved from bombed buildings was stored in large warehouses. You could pick out items of clothing and furniture to help you get through the hard times.

Along with some furniture, her mother picked up a Singer treadle. Mother found that she had a talent for sewing and soon started to earn extra income making dresses and doing alterations. Times were tough but laughter and determination saw them through. Incidents that we would see as strange today, were often laughed about.

There was the time when a Doodlebug exploded and the engine landed in the street outside their new house. While Mary's dad was at work her brother, who was nine, got his father's toolkit out and started to take the engine apart. Much to the amusement of the MOD chaps that had come to cart it away for examination.

There were also sad times. Mary remembers one incident as clearly as if it had happened yesterday. When her mother had finished a wedding dress it was her job to take it across London and deliver it. Mary did her best not to get a single mark on it. Five shillings was the price of the dress. Enough to feed the family and buy coal for a week.

It was a beautiful white lace and satin dress with beads running around the neckline and a lining made from parachute silk that had been acquired on the black market. When Mary arrived at the house she eagerly rang the bell and waited. As she saw the dress the young woman who opened the door burst into tears.

Her fiancé had been killed in action on the beaches of France.

Mary took the dress back home crying all the way. No money meant no supper either. The coalman was told that no coal was needed that week and was sent on his way. Mary and her brother stared at the empty fireplace on the cold nights wrapped in blankets.

On more than one occasion during this terrible period they found a sack of coal leaning against the back door. Though they were grateful never a word was spoken, none was needed.

Times were tough but things eased as her mother became better known for her sewing. One of Mary's strongest memories of her mother was the sound of the treadle as its rhythmical motion rocked her to sleep. She would often wake to the sound in the morning.

During the 1950s rationing hit home – almost worse than the war years. Many young women had already taken the opportunity to escape the poverty and travelled to America to start a new life with their serviceman. About 70,000 women married US soldiers, sailors and airmen. During the war years in Britain, around 25,000 new babies came into the world with

American servicemen as their fathers.

It was a sore point with many of the British lads at the time. That's when the saying started: *There are only three things wrong with American servicemen: They are over-paid, oversexed and over here.*

Many fought the war and returned home to find their loved ones going off to the *Promised Land.* It was not just Americans, there were servicemen here from all over the world. 100,000 Polish had escaped from Hitler's blitzcreig and made their way to England.

Mary was far too young for all this to affect her but one day her pretty neighbour disappeared in an American staff car, never to return.

One day, after school, Mary was taken on a surprise trip. It ended at the local sewing-machine shop. There was a brand new Harris sewing machine at the shop with a scarlet ribbon wrapped around it. On the case was her name. Secretly her mother had being making payments on the machine each month for her birthday.

It was the best present she had ever received and that evening she took huge pride in mending the gusset of her father's work trousers. Her father, in turn, took great pains to try them on and see what a wonderful job his daughter had done. He bent up and down pretending to be at work picking up tickets from the floor of his bus.

Mary Wilding still uses that same hand-operated Harris. She would never contemplate using anything else. I was called in to service the machine and bring it back to its former glory. This was when she shared part of her life with me. She misses those years when everyone pulled together but not the cold nights after the coalman was sent away for another week when they all wore three lots of clothing and stared at an empty fireplace.

Another typical country lane, just wide enough for a tractor. The South Downs are in the distance

My son Tom moments before collecting water from the 'Malvern Hills' which turned into a water fight.

A weather beaten tree in the snow that has had to put up with the high winds off the English channel.

LEDBURY WITH THE IN-LAWS

After a splendid hot summer and a great tourist season the weather suddenly changed.

Most of our tourists returned home to dream of breakfast in a Victorian seaside hotel. Although repairs were buoyant, sewing machines sales had been poor during the holiday season.

We are surrounded by chain stores selling very cheap, in both sense of the word, sewing machines. That hits the sales of new machines. Why spend double the price on a new Frister & Rossmann when another machine looks just as good? It is only when they try to sew that the difference becomes clear. The old saying *You only get what you pay for* is certainly true where sewing machines are concerned.

I took advantage of the quiet spell before the run up to Christmas to get away for a few days. We packed the family up and headed off to Hereford, a part of England that seems forever in a different time. I stroked the granite top of King John's coffin in Worcester Cathedral and wondered if he ever cursed Robin Hood. He was a king who had fought with just about everybody his entire life. A devious king by all accounts, he tried to cheat his brother, Richard the Lionheart, out of his throne while Richard was away on the crusades. He even argued with the Pope and was excommunicated. Right up until the day he died in 1216, before he was 50, he was engaged in a bitter civil war.

King John was not all bad. He signed Magna Carta that ultimately meant that people were better off than they had been since 1066. He also threw the French invaders out of Rye, one of my favourite towns just along the coast from us.

We walked the old cobbled streets of Malvern, set below the Malvern Hills that dominate the area, where the street lamps are still lit by gas. The Queen gets her water from the Malvern Hills. It runs sweet and clear from the hillside, packed full of minerals. We collected a few pints until Tom, our son decided to splash it everywhere and water collecting turned into a water fight.

As a family, including all the in-laws, we booked into a small hotel-come-pub in Ledbury, called The Talbot. It is a lovely oak hostelry built around 1550. The building, that has settled with time, is as crooked as a dog's hind leg. You can get seasick walking along the twisting corridors. The mother-in-law tripped several times but we put that down to the local brew she was drinking. The oak-beamed ceilings are low, built for people centuries ago, who rarely grew to five feet. The hotel is so picturesque and it fits in neatly with the pretty, English market town.

A large cheerful man ran the pub. He had a face the size of a frying pan and a smile just as wide. He worked all day behind the bar, serving lovely hop-rich beer brewed in the area and making strangers feel welcome. "A stranger is just a friend I 'av' not met yet" he told me.

He seemed tireless and seldom got to bed before three am. I knew this for his weight on the old floorboards made them creak as he made his way to a room near ours. The first night I sat up in bed thinking I was getting a visit from a ghost. It was pitch black and the footsteps came closer and closer to my door much to my astonishment then seemed to lift above and walk straight over to me.

What was happening was that he slept in the room above us. In the dark it sounded as if he was walking straight to me. By the end of the week I was accustomed to his slow, heavy tread and I felt familiar with it.

We ate breakfast each morning in the dining room. It had been the site of a minor engagement between Oliver Cromwell's Roundheads and King Charles' Cavaliers. I sat mesmerised by the old room where the sound of steel blades would have echoed through the corridors. All this was happening not long after the Founding Fathers had set sail aboard the Mayflower to America and the promise of spiritual freedom. One hundred and two Pilgrims crammed on board a 90-foot wine boat had made a desperate escape to a new land.

Amazingly the first Indian that they came into contact with spoke English. He was an escaped slave that had learnt his master's language. This chance meeting, that many say was God's work, led to the Pilgrims giving thanks and in 1621 the great American tradition of Thanksgiving was born.

One wall of the dining room consisted mostly of a large fireplace where dough for bread, would have been left to rise and where hogs would have been roasted on the spit. The entire wood-panelled wall surrounding the fireplace was engraved with scenes from a bygone age, perhaps of that trip to America.

The whole of the Hereford area is prime farming country. During the days we walked through fields of gold as pheasant ran from their hiding-places safe in the high summer corn. We stopped at many tearooms, they were hard to pass. The thought of lovely cream teas, of scones and butter with lashings of strawberry jam and cream made them all impossible to miss. I must have put on a stone!

The whole family had a great time. We missed Grampy Cyril not being with us. At the age of 88 he had passed away and gone to the great gardener's paradise in the sky.

Cyril had been a part of my life since the first day we met nearly 20 years earlier. When my wife first introduced us she said, "Don't talk to him very long as he is frail and you must not make him any weaker. He is going to die any day now."

Well, for another 20 years he proved everyone wrong.

Cyril was someone very special, the perfect old man. He never upset anyone and was always there when you needed someone to talk to. He would tell me tales of life in Eastbourne from yesteryear. Like when Kings Drive, the main road into town was just a dirt track and where the Grand Hotel on the seafront grew its own vegetables for its restaurant. He told me of the times, as a child, when he would run to the beach to watch the bi-planes having dogfights over the coast and when airships were a common sight, moored near Eastbourne at the present site of Willingdon Community College, full of passengers bound for the continent.

The endless hours we passed in idle chat were priceless. I probably learned more from Cyril than any man I have ever met. He had the art, the secret of age. Perhaps in all his years working with the soil he had learnt the secret of life itself. A few weeks before his death, as we sat together, he put his hand on my leg and looked at me. We said nothing but we both knew it was goodbye.

After he passed away I sat and wrote my favourite poem about someone very special. I hope one day that we will meet again. I called it *Tiny Acorns*.

Grampy and Spike hard at work. John Cyril Gordon Cottington – Grampy! He was responsible as head gardener for Eastbourne Council for the preparation of thousands of plants. These plants kept the beautiful carpet gardens looking tip top for years. Grampy took over from his brother who in turn took over from their father and in turn his father before. Eastbourne's flowers had been grown by Yana's family for over a century. When Cyril first cycled along Kings Drive to work it was a gravel track.

1920's Eastbourne
John Cottingham in his hat, jacket and tie putting the finishing touches to the carpet gardens. During the growing season he would grow over $1/2$ million geraniums.

Jack Reed, Yana's great grandfather, 4th from the left worked for Eastbourne Railway in the Victorian era. Note the very early engines behind. Yana's maternal grandparents the Reed's and the Cottington's were both old Eastbourne families. Working families that helped in their way to shape the Eastbourne we know today.

The main Kings Drive nursery known as Clifton Nursery hit by German bombs. It did not matter much as during the war most of the beautiful flower beds in Eastbourne were turned over for vegetables.

Nelson Reed, Yana's great uncle. Nelson enlisted under age in the same Lowther Lambs regiment as Rudyard Kipling's son in WW1. Nelson like untold numbers met an untimely end in the muddy Flanders fields. The posthumous medals were of little comfort to his grieving family.

TINY ACORNS

I hear the birdsong as autumn leaves lay like a chestnut sea.
And gaze with saddened eyes while gentle rain entrances me.
So swift the seasons run this year, so soon the swallows fly,
While church bells toll to summon all for a friend has passed us by.

Oh how the tears do swell with the choir in harmony,
Where angels dwell in every note and where my friend should be.
I dare not glance at others eyes should I feel their pain in me,
This death has shaken all our souls with cold reality.

We stout men of England strong, that grew from soil so rich,
That beat the anvils from our past and learnt their rhythmic pitch,
We walked the path of duty to earn our right to stay,
Yet beneath the churchyard yew is where we grudging lay.

What happened to those sunny days and our endless schemes,
When we were tiny acorns amongst a field of dreams?
Wide-eyed we raced through life with our hearts brimming full,
But the final flag is a shroud of silk so harsh and miserable.

Were I to take your hand my friend, were I to grasp it hard,
I'd gladly share half my days though it would mark my card,
Then through the lofty corridors where silent whispers fly,
We'd shout our voices hoarse my friend and laugh until we die.

Alex. I. Askaroff

BACK TO WORK

Well, the holiday, like most things, was soon over. We came back to the real world.

At work my first call of the day was to replace the motor of a Frister & Rossmann with a new one. This was well worth doing and my customer was doing a happy dance. When I left she was still playing with her 21st birthday present that was now forty years old.

I then had to replace the motor on an industrial Husqvarna. This was a heavy, slow, sweaty job but, after three cups of tea and a couple of hours of hard toil, it was sewing beautifully. Then a few minor repairs and back to base to answer the phone messages. My holiday was still strong in my mind. Boy, it was hard to get back into work mode.

On my way home, late in the morning, I was still half on holiday and half daydreaming when I passed Shermans Bridge on the main Eastbourne to Brighton road. I suddenly remembered one of the funniest incidents that had ever happened to me.

When we were kids, my Dad, Igor – what a great Russian name – would often take us out for a drive. This would allow Mumsie to cook the Sunday roast in peace and not have six annoying boys running amok around her apron strings. On one of these drives my younger brother, Simon, needed to go to the toilet. It was a quiet Sunday morning so Dad stopped the car on the main road right next to Shermans Bridge.

We all, including Dad, got out and took up positions along the bridge like a row of boy-soldiers awaiting further instructions. Almost simultaneously we all started to pee over the side of the bridge doing a good impression of an Italian fountain into the River Cuckmere some twenty feet below. At the end of the row, close to the bank, I was happily gazing at a stream of gold as it cut the morning air feeling that special sense of relief that children get from an overdue pee.

Suddenly I heard muttering from below me, that started to erupt into screaming. "What! What the hell! What the ******* hell is going on?"

I looked down below me where the pee was heading and where all the noise was coming from. Directly underneath me there was a fisherman, on the bank, being sprayed with my frothy concoction. In total shock I could not stop! It was going everywhere now. All over his fishing box, over the cap he was wearing and over him. He was twisting and slipping. Trying to get away from my wet and rude donation to his Sunday morning's fishing.

He must have been half asleep on a peaceful Sunday morning watching his float bobbing up and down in the slow quiet waters of the river. That was before we turned up and all hell broke loose.

My Dad shouted to us, "Run for it boys, back to the car!"

We were all rushing in complete panic, trying to finish what does not stop easily when you are young.

The fisherman was swearing like a prisoner who had just slipped on the soap in the showers. He was clambering up the side of the bank trying to get to us. We were all crushing into the one door that was open on the side of the car, not stopping to think that it would be much quicker opening another door.

We burned off up the road as fast as we could. I was looking out of the rear window only to see the fisherman, shaking his fists in wild fury, standing in the middle of the road. A mile up the road the silence in the car exploded into laughter. Dad had to stop because we were all laughing so hard that he could not drive for the tears in his eyes.

It was an accident, a collision of fate. No harm was meant. We could never pass that bridge again without laughing at the poor fisherman's misfortune. Back at home Dad tried to tell me off in front of Mumsie but he started laughing so much, retelling his tale, that we all started again and ended up with stomach cramps. I would have given anything to hear the fisherman's explanation to his wife when he got home. It was simply one of the funniest things I have ever seen.

One of our more successful pike sorties. As usual Tom caught the pike, he is the luckiest fisherman I know.

Harry Allchorn, a famous name in Eastbourne. The Allchorn's have been part of Eastbourne Lifeguards and Lifeboat since Victorian times. They ran the pleasure boats on the seafront for 60 years. Presently there are still two lifeguard Allchorn's on Eastbourne beaches. Harry pictured was nicknamed Early Doors! In 1944 when this picture was taken he was working the fishing boats hence the state of his jacket. Harry is holding Annette and her cousin Marlene (who is the mother-in-law) is smiling sweetly by the pram. Even with war raging there was time for fun.

153

A SUMMER SYMPHONY

Tugged by a passing breeze the porch door softly opened,

Entering our silence the idle chattering of garden birds fell upon my ears.

Sweet breaths of summer thought I, stay awhile and bring your noisy friends,

Remind me of meadows ripe and dusty trails winding through forgotten valleys.

Let me hear the easy laughter that flows from country pubs on lazy afternoons,

Of sun kissed children saving sandcastles on ice cream beaches,

Come my forgotten friend whisk me through the ether, back to

Confetti swirling around church doorways as you lift the bells aloft,

To chilled lemonade and cucumber sandwiches in willow hampers.

Tell me of how you ruffle the parasols draping distant verandas

While white flannel trousers and Panama hats seduce French laced lovers.

Come my welcome visitor and whisper to me of these things that so enrich life,

And gently ease me back to sleep with a summer symphony.

A.I.A

MISSION IN A MICRA

What a morning! I was late leaving for work due to a leak in the roof that kept me up half the night.

The car I was using was a new Nissan Micra. It was on loan while my beautiful Land Rover Discovery was being repaired. It had been smashed up quite badly when an old boy pulled straight across the main carriageway without looking. It is one of the problems that comes from living in a very old community.

I think the average age of drivers in Eastbourne is about 103!

"I could not see a thing, blooming sign's in the way," he muttered as he examined the damage to my car.

Anyway, off I went in my mini-Micra, the engine squealing like a finely tuned rubber band. I was halfway to my first call in Seddlescombe, some 25 miles from home, when I spotted a family of wild deer running along the edge of Ashburnham Forest. In the golden morning light they were picked out against the trees in a timeless scene. Forgetting I was in the Micra I pulled up to the kerb to take a photo. This would have been no problem in my Discovery but the Micra decided the huge, almost three-inch, kerb was not mountable. The result was I scraped the wheel-cover on my loan car that had only done 30 miles from new. I could just imagine the face of the garage owner when I returned. They had made such a fuss over checking it with me and then I had to sign for it in triplicate. I thought maybe I should just throw the cover away and tell them it was not fitted properly.

Arriving late at my first call I promptly serviced a lovely Bernina Record 830, one of the finest machines ever to come out of the Swiss factory. I do love working on these fine pieces of engineering. Undoing every screw is a pleasure. The name Bernina comes from one of the most beautiful mountains in the Swiss Alps, just thought I would throw that in for you.

I was no sooner finished than the owner pulled out a poor Jones. I fixed this and grabbed my tools, now being an hour behind schedule. "Hold on a second young man. Could you just have a look over this old Singer?" She took me into the garage and, with a deft arm movement, removed a sheet covering a neglected Singer 201k. I sighed. If it were any other I would have left it. But a 201k? I just had to save it.

She told me how she had had two other engineers look at it but they had failed to fix it. It had not worked properly for over 20 years. It was her favourite machine having been bought by her dad in 1951, Singer's centenary year. He had had to order it and wait 18 months for delivery.

Within 35 minutes it was sewing like new. The other engineers, if they were engineers, missed a really obvious tension failure that only occurred each time the foot was raised and lowered.

Later than ever, I bombed off to Hastings with "Bless you!" ringing in my ears. I had my foot flat on the floor. I had to get some miles behind me but in the Micra I could have gone faster if I put my feet out and ran.

My next call was a gear replacement. Another time consuming job. In addition I had the help of Kyle, an 18-month-old baby, who obviously thought he was my assistant. He seemed to think that trying to swallow most of my tool kit was the best way to fix his mum's machine.

Once finished I made my farewells to Kyle promising to pick him up in 20 years to finish off his training. I was on a roll and sped off to Bexhill as fast as my bean can could go. I still had no time to stop for a coffee and a headache was presenting itself in a *told-you-so* manner.

My next customer was a gem. No sooner had I fixed her machine, a 1970's Singer, than she asked me to look at her electric chair. I had a few thoughts about what she meant running through my head but said nothing. An hour later she was sitting in her chair being lifted up and down her stairs, smiling like a kid. She rummaged around in her old purse and produced a ten-pound note, then promptly asked for change. I had none so she kept it I missed out on a tip. Never mind she was happy.

Over the years I have fixed many things that have nothing to do with sewing machines. Everything from boilers to lathes. Looking back on the last call, I spent twice as much time on the chair as the sewing machine and got nothing more for it than a smile. Mind you a smile can make one's day.

The last customer of the morning was pacing up and down her living room waiting for me. She made me take my shoes off but thought nothing of her two golden retrievers making a mess everywhere. She then promptly went on to tell me how she used to kill chickens. Strange woman I thought as I beavered away on her machine.

Still, she had a nice Riccar electronic multi-stitch. It was the machine's first service in 19 years so you can imagine the mess. At last I had time to have a coffee, which poured into my veins directly bypassing my intestinal tract. The only bad thing about stopping for a break was that I had to hear more about killing things.

"Used to shoot 'em with the old man's rifle. Straight between the eyes," were the last words she uttered as I headed for my rented *elastic-band* parked in her drive. I left with visions of chickens running for their lives as the mad old bat took aim over the farm gate.

By now it was lunchtime and I was thrashing the blue-beast home across the Pevensey Levels. "Home James!" I shouted to the *elastic-band*, "And don't spare the horses – both of them."

The car surged forward to an eager 40 miles per hour, spurred on by my foot that was trying to push the accelerator through the floor. I had all my toolboxes strapped in, like children on the seats, as there was not enough room in the boot. The engine howled and objected but I showed no mercy. Oh how I longed for my lovely, faithful, Land Rover!

These are the deer I stopped to photograph in the story 'Mission in a Micra'

No one knows who carved the 230ft giant into the hillside at Wilmington. It could be a victorian folly, others say it has much older pagan roots.

The flooding in Autumn was not all bad news, these swans (The Queen's birds) took advantage of the flooded Pevensey marshes. It was here in 1066 that William the Conqueror landed.

NESTA'S STORY

Nesta Harmer, one of my customers kindly told me this story that starts way back in the Victorian era.

Nesta was the granddaughter of Fredrick Richard Watson, a senior NCO serving in the British Army. This story is about FR Watson, his wife, their second child, Freda (Nesta's mother) and of course, Nesta.

It is also the story of her grandmother's Singer sewing machine and how it played a small but important part throughout their lives.

FR Watson joined the Royal Artillery in the British Army while Queen Victoria ruled one third of the entire world. Her armies policed the four corners of the earth. Her subjects were kept under control by a vast and well-organised military machine and the sun truly never set on her empire.

Fredrick joined as a boy and worked his way up through the ranks in what is now Pakistan. By 1894 Fred was married and had the first of 5 children, all born wherever they happened to be serving around the globe.

In 1896 after the birth of Freda orders were dispatched to England to ship a sewing machine out to them on the Northwest Frontier, where the railway was pushing forward. Once the Singer arrived Nesta's grandmother made all her children's clothes on her machine. To make it more convenient for travelling a special case was made to allow the Singer to be strapped to a horse.

Nesta's grandmother also had an ayah to help with the children, our equivalent of a nanny. She would often turn the sewing machine handle while Nesta's grandmother sewed. I can just imagine the scene now as they co-ordinated perfectly to sew a seam!

Nesta's grandfather was a brilliant horseman. He would lead his troop up into the Himalayas finding new routes from Islamabad into the mountains and the Northwest Passage. In their troop were infantrymen, cavalry, artillery, cooks, a doctor, medical staff, workmen, cleaners, servants and teams of pack animals loaded to the hilt. An entire community that was self-sufficient for weeks at a time.

On one push forward up the Peshawar, into the mountains, the horse carrying the Singer tripped and fell from the path down the Khudside. It was badly injured and had to be shot (and eaten later, the bones and hooves being boiled to make glue). That was the reality of life at the time. They lived with hardships on a daily basis, overcoming them and moving on.

The sewing machine was taken to the local fundi, a repairman found on many village streets. He would have the ability to repair just about anything. To the locals he was an essential part of the community and was held in high esteem. They say that the fundi has *magic in his hands*. Perhaps I am Eastbourne's equivalent to the fundi as many times customers have told me I have magic hands. Although the fundi had probably never seen a sewing machine before he managed to make repairs that, 40 years later, were still holding well.

The family survived many trips and many countries, growing all the time. The machine stayed with them as part of the family. It was in constant use making and repairing for the five children, doing uniform repairs and endless other tasks.

Occasionally special silks were sent for and gowns were made for the officer's ball. The ball was the highlight of the year and the officers' wives were expected to sparkle. The Singer survived sea journeys, long treks across mountains and high altitudes. It travelled with the Watson family wherever they were serving.

From their base at Portsmouth the family moved around. From India to Malta, Ireland and many other places. By the outbreak of the Great War Fredrick had three pips on his shoulder and had become senior gunnery officer. Not bad for a young lad who had started at the bottom of the British Army cleaning shoes.

After a bloody battle in Flanders, Belgium, Fredrick was captured by the Hun and taken to a prison camp. Once he was located, his wife would make up parcels and the Red Cross would usually deliver them. Basic clothing, once again sewn on the trusty old Singer, would make its way to his camp. At the camp Fred had been given the code name *Micky Dripping* and was chairman of the Escape Committee. Meanwhile, Nesta's grandmother managed to join the Red Cross in Switzerland to do her part during the war and be a little closer to Fredrick.

One of the items they made and sent out to him was a chair. The wooden frame was much like a deck chair and the fabric was from a worn Turkish rug they had cut up and sewn together, once again on the good old Singer. It was crude but tough.

Many years later, while out for a picnic with her mother and grandmother on Wandsworth Common in London, Nesta was sitting in the deck chair, the one that had come back with her grandad from prison camp. A passer-by stopped and stared at the chair, seemingly mesmerised. He came up and introduced himself. He was a fellow inmate and officer at the same prison camp as Fredrick Watson. He had often sat in the very same chair, talking in whispered tones with Micky Dripping of escape from the dreaded Hun.

In the thirties Nesta's grandmother took her faithful Singer in to the local Singer dealer to have it serviced. Intrigued by the strange packing-box and well-used look the dealer enquired about the machine's history. Nesta's grandmother related some of it over a cup of tea in the back of the store. The dealer just had to have the machine.

After a lot of horse-trading at which Nesta's grandmother was extremely deft, he gave her a brand new Singer model 99 in exchange for her beaten-up old machine. Her Singer then went on display in the proud dealer's front window, complete with its story.

Nesta still sews on her new Singer 99 passed down from her grandmother to her mother and to her. She won't have a motor put on it, *None of that modern stuff,* and she loves it dearly, telling me that it will see her out. She has an excellent memory of so many of the stories her grandmother told her about life over a century before. Stories of how one little Singer sewing machine followed their lives around the world.

If she closes her eyes really tight she can still see granny, back in 1920 at the end of hostilities with Germany. She is sewing brand-new bright floral curtains for senior NCO Fredrick Richard Watson's homecoming. Yes, Micky Dripping was coming home.

Rolly, my dog on 'the secret beach' in Eastbourne. Behind are the huge cliffs that stand like a great castle wall protecting England.

The Pilgrims' Rest, Battle, one of the oldest houses in Battle and haunted!

CURTAIN CAPERS

A ghost story from Battle

Battle is steeped in history and, today, survives in a time-warp. A great abbey that was built a thousand years ago dominates the top end of the High Street. Battle gets its name from a turning point in British history. You guessed it, from a battle!

The year is 1066. King Edward dies and leaves a weak county and many broken promises. In Norway a Viking king greedy for power has his eye set on our land. He assembles a huge army and sets sail for northern England. In the south Harold Godwinsson is quickly crowned and sets off to get rid of this Norwegian upstart in cahoots with his half brother.

A bloody battle ensued at Stamford Bridge near York and Harold is victorious, killing both would be usurpers. Before he can turn around another foreigner was up to no good. William, Duke of Normandy was invading in the south. William had also been promised the throne by the recently departed Edward. Some say Harold also offered it to him when in France, but I doubt it.

Harold gathered his weakened army and marched at full speed across England to meet William. Harold and his army marched 250 miles in thirteen days. One of the most impressive forced marches in history. William had landed at Pevensey Bay unopposed. He built a makeshift castle in Hastings and started to march towards London. The last successful invasion of England had begun.

However things were not going to be easy. Harold caught him by surprise and brought his army down on William's a few miles north of Hastings.

Two great armies faced each other along a ridge, later to be named Senlac – sea of blood. Harold's men outnumbered the French by over two thousand but they were tired from fighting and marching.

This great turning point in British history is full of questions. By far the biggest is *why did Harold not have his archers with him?* They were lightly equipped and would have been easier to move the distance from York. It would be the same as a modern army not having their rifles.

Although Harold had the high ground and more men, they were easy pickings for the French archers. At one stage the battle almost stopped because William had to send for more arrows. Normally the opposition would soon return the arrows shot at them. In this battle it could not happen.

The Normans had a very different way of fighting than the Anglo Saxon English. The English were armed with swords, spears and large two-handed axes. They fought much as they had done for centuries, having been influenced by the Vikings. They rode to battle but always fought on foot. Their horses were far too precious to lose in battle.

The Normans on the other hand were a modern army. Using battle horses to mow down and break up the foot soldiers for the archers to kill at a distance. They were far more mobile and thought about their strategies during the conflict, altering them as needed.

Slowly Harold's men were struck down. Then William faked a charge on both Harold's flanks and retreated. Harold's flanks, thinking the Normans were in retreat, charged down from their ridge and chased them. Suddenly they found themselves surrounded, counter-attacked and slaughtered.

Nevertheless, the battle raged on all day with no clear winner. Rumours were rife of William's death. At one point William rode through his men with his helmet off so they could see he was still alive.

Then things changed. Legend tells that one of the arrows struck Harold in the eye leaving him alive but mortally wounded. William, expecting surrender, thought the day was his.

This was not to be. Harold's finest men, his Housecarl, surrounded the King, picked him up and fell back to the highest point of Senlac ridge.

William had no option but to keep fighting into the evening. Not one of King Harold's personal guards surrendered. They fought on even as the remains of Harold's army fled, scattering into the night. As the last rays of light left the battlefield Harold, his brothers Gyrth and Leofwine and many of his personal guard lay dead. For each of Harold's guards that fell, five enemy soldiers lay around them. The ground was soaked in blood.

Later that night Harold's mother pleaded with William to allow her son a proper burial, even offering William her son's weight in gold – but she was denied. Harold's mutilated body was identified by his common-law wife Edith Swan-Neck and spirited off for secret burial. Some say on the shores of Hastings seafront.

William brought up his priests and they gave thanks to God for their victory.

After the battle William had a huge fire built and spent the night on the battlefield alone with the dead and dying. He gave thanks to God and vowed to keep the promise he had made before the battle. William later ordered a great Abbey to be built on the site where Harold died.

So started the town of Battle and a turning point in our history.

Stories of the ghost of Harold still abound. He was last seen by a schoolboy, back in 1972, standing in full armour near the Abbey gazing out towards the battlefield. In spring locals say the fields still run red with the blood of the fallen. This is partially true because occasionally the fields do seem to have blood coming from them. Specialists have put this down to the high iron content of the area that seeps out as red rust.

England was won in a day and the face of our country changed. Over the following decades dozens of castles and hundreds of Norman church towers stretched across our soil. Although it was to be another five years before Hereward fled, the country belonged to William.

The history of England changed from the shadowy Dark Ages that had been with us since the departure of the Romans to one of strength and great kings – to crusades and splendid tales of knights and damsels.

Never again did the English repeat their mistake of coming against the enemy without archers. In 1415 Henry V with 6000 men was cornered near Calais in northern France by 25,000 troops. He won a resounding victory. They slaughtered more than 10,000, and wiped out the flower of the French aristocracy for the loss of less than 500 English. The battle of Agincourt was testament to the English bowmen and how important they were in war.

The town of Battle is much today as it was centuries ago. A traveller or pilgrim making his way from the coast, perhaps on a pilgrimage to St Thomas Becket's shrine at Canterbury or another monastery, would recognise it instantly. The Pilgrims Rest in front of the Abbey still serves good wholesome food under the same oak beams that have burnt black from the open fires of centuries past. Fittingly enough at the moment it is French cuisine that is served.

One evening I had a phone call from a lady in Battle who was obviously in a state of shock. I could feel her shaking down the phone. She asked if there was any reason that her sewing machine should start sewing on its own. I explained there was several things that could make a machine misbehave in this way and arranged to have a look at it later in the week.

Her house lay in the shadow of Battle Abbey and she ushered me in to the drawing room where a pretty Singer 99 sat on the table. I examined the foot control, no problem there. The wiring was clean but on inspecting the motor I found that the suppresser had shorted out causing the motor to run by itself.

I removed the offending item and showed Mrs Bailey the suppresser. She kept turning it over in her hands asking if I was positive that this was the problem. Then she told me why she was upset.

In the drawing room over the leaded-glass windows hung some bright, almost tacky-looking, curtains. The sort of thing that would remind you of a London fruit market. Mrs Bailey hated those curtains but her husband loved them so they agreed to disagree. However time rolled on and poor Mr Bailey popped his clogs. He has only been in the ground a week, hardly had a chance to push up the daisies, when Mrs Bailey whips up the street to the local haberdashery shop and buys new curtain material.

She cut out the curtains then heaved the trusty old Singer 99 out of the cellar and proceeded to sew them up. As the evening drew on she decided to have a break and made herself a lovely cup of Earl Grey tea.

The phone rang and she answered it. As she was chatting to her friend, a cuppa in one hand and phone in the other, she became aware of a noise coming out of the drawing room. She glanced across into the dark room where the only light was the one on her sewing machine. To her horror, the new curtain was moving through the machine by itself!

Frightened stiff she dropped her tea and the phone.

Convinced that her hubby had come back to get her for changing his favourite curtains she approached the machine. The foot did not respond and the curtain was moving faster. That's when she unplugged the machine and then shaking like a leaf in an autumn storm, contacted me.

I fixed the machine and gave it a good service. As I left she was still examining the suppresser with a suspicious look. Many years passed before I was called back to service the machine. I could not help but notice that she still had her old curtains up and I commented on them. She told me that while the machine was behaving itself she was not going to tempt fate and change them just in case it was her husband that had come back to haunt her after all.

Many a stranger thing may have happened in Battle.

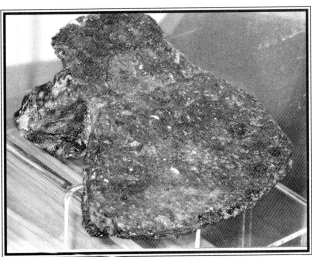

This plain looking piece of rusty metal has a fascinating and bloody history.
It is a warrior's axe head unearthed near Senlac Ridge. Senlac (sea of blood) Ridge was the site of England's most famous battle and turning point in history, the Battle of Hastings. There is little doubt that an Anglo Saxon warrior in the battle wielded this battle-axe. No warriour would leave such a valuable weapon. The chances are that he, like thousands of others on that day, died defending his country in ferocious hand-to-hand combat. All that is left to remind us of that extraordinary day of the death, screams and carnage is this rusty piece of metal.
(Photograph with kind permission of Battle Museum).

COUNTRY WAYS – AUTUMN

I set off, as usual, on my sewing-machine repair rounds. The Land Rover loaded to the hilt with tools and equipment. First stop to a water-damaged Gamages special, a 1960s straight-stitch machine.

Gamages was a large department store that sold so many sewing machines that they had their own name on them. This one had been in the floods and then left in a basement. The shuttle had seized but after a bit of persuasion with some WD-40 and copious amounts of elbow grease it came grunting back to life. Before long the stitch was perfect. Money changed hands and I was off.

I went inland, up towards Burwash and Rudyard Kipling-land. Burwash is a part of the country that is so English. Cream teas and thatched cottage land. It is almost into Kent and on the ridge, you can see the oast-houses that were used for drying out the hops. They look like giant Amish women marching across the land with their dark wooden skirts and white caps.

Many used to refer to Kent as *The Garden of England*. It was beautiful. As beautiful as ever a place on earth could be. There is also something so quaint about the area that is easy on the eye.

Near Burwash I met an old acquaintance, a stockbroker, who had retired down from London a few years back. As I fixed his wife's Frister & Rossmann Cub he told me how he started at the bottom of the Stock Exchange, in the City, forty years earlier. While I fixed the machine, the tension had collapsed, I heard how he worked his way up the greasy pole from a Blue Button's runner's-runner (lowest of the low apparently, close to a snail) to be the Chairman of the Board.

He had spent a lifetime without ever touching a screwdriver, paintbrush or ladder. At 65 he had to learn how the rest of the world lived and worked, not how to open six bottles of Bollinger at a party. He was enjoying every second of it.

For my next call I wriggled my way down the wet country lanes towards

Framfield. I found a spot to park for a short break in a heavily wooded area and watched autumn in all her glory. A beautiful jay dropped out of the forest onto the oak tree that opened above me like a great umbrella with no cloth. It skipped from branch to branch, grabbed an acorn and disappeared into the woods all in a matter of seconds.

The jay, which is the most colourful of all the crow family, was always a sight to behold. I probably only saw a dozen Jay's a year and each one was a pleasure, especially around mating time when their screeching cries echo around the Sussex woodlands. They often make a laughing sound a bit like a magpie's that mimics a chuckle. However once nesting they become almost silent with just low crooning warbles to entice their mates. In the autumn, they gather and hoard their favourite fruits, the acorns.

They say that if it were not for the jay's planting of the acorns much of the natural forests of oak would never have grown.

Hedge sparrows were noisily fighting over the last shiny-black ivy berries that clung to the dying foliage. In the breeze the bare branches of the hedgerows were scratching angrily at a darkening sky. Ferns that had been a vibrant green all summer had turned deep reddish-brown as they have done every year since the time that mammoths strode these lands.

The roads were paved with fallen leaves in a thousand autumn shades. Water was running across my path in newly-formed streams, making its way down to the sea some many miles away. The whole countryside was sodden and in its shabbiest overcoat but still full of life.

Squirrels were busily collecting horse chestnuts and acorns, ready for the lean winter months ahead. It would not be long before conkers would be played by thousands of schoolboys in schoolyards across rural England.

*****

Conkers was one of those games when I was young that has almost disappeared today. Basically it was little more than a conker hanging on a string that would be walloped by another conker, however there was more, much more. Some conkers became almost legendary and hunted down like Jessie James.

Imagine the school playground at break time, loads of boys all gathered around a circle with the two combatants facing each other. One boy, with tongue tightly wedged in the side of his mouth and a fixed stare of concentration in his eyes, would swipe his conker at another's conker hoping to dislodge or smash the latter.

If he missed it was his tough luck, if he tangled the strings he would forfeit another shot unless the playground rules were abandoned. Then he could tug with all his might and try to pull the conker from his opponent. If he managed to dislodge it a shout of stamps would go up and if the opponent was not quick enough his conker would end up as a mushy lump crushed into the schoolyard tarmac by the shoe of the victor.

Occasionally a perfect line-up shot would crack down on the opponents conker sending it shattering to the floors in bits, cheers and whoops would rip through the onlookers. If the smashed conker had been a good one and broken several others before its demise the victor would add the number of the vanquished conker to his own. In this way school champions were made and startlingly high numbers were achieved. These conkers were prime targets for all the other children for if your conker could smash the champion you became *number one* in the playground. I once had a conker that made it to 67 before cracked and wounded it succumbed to a windmill smash from Chris Higgins's monster. He cried for joy, I just cried.

The best conker trees were a well-guarded secret and dawn raids often organised, especially after a storm when many prize conkers littered the ground. Armed with heavy sticks kids would attack the helpless trees trying to knock down the green shells that held the magnificent brown conkers. Opening the shells though sometimes difficult and often painful would sporadically yield a prize specimen that made your eyes pop out of your head. Examining a brown beauty would bring images of future victory to mind.

Once procured ancient remedies were used to harden conkers, baking in a slow oven, soaking in vinegar, storing in the airing cupboard, many sneaky methods employed to ensure a pocket full of super hard conkers were stuffed in the school blazer each morning.

Conker time at school was a great time and for a few weeks all participants

of the glorious game could be easily recognised by their bruised knuckles and red fingers.

*****

I pulled up outside Pump Cottage and was greeted by an enthusiastic large Lurcher and a ginger tomcat. By the doorknocker hung two pheasant. I leaned over and sniffed them to see how long they had been hanging. They smelled of the countryside and the fresh earth so they must have been shot that morning. It would be a few days before the familiar smell that country people wait for appears. Only then would they be plucked then roasted and served with a plate-full of roast potatoes and fresh vegetables.

I had been to the cottage five years earlier and remembered the old Jones machine that had been worked hard mending everything from the hubby's overalls to the children's Halloween costumes. It was in a well-used state and took some time to bring back to life.

The Lurcher was stretched out on the settee, and reminded me of a drunken lord basking by the fire, lazily gazing at the tail of the ginger tom that twitched nearby. It's a hard life I thought.

Then off to a caravan park to a little old lady who had returned from Spain with an ailing Alfa. The Alfa was in a beautiful honey-beech cabinet, small and compact and inlaid with different coloured woods. She had bought it from Estapona and, although it was made in the 1950s, was in superb condition.

In the drawer was a De Reszke cigarette tin, now used for keeping pins. On the side of the tin, next to a rather spiffing gentleman with a monocle, it proudly announced Cigarettes to the Aristocracy.

The poor old dear had had a stroke awhile back and I had taught her how to sew with a treadle again. It took some time but, in the end, she clicked and off she went like a kid on her first bike. The treadle rocking away happily to her foot movements. The clickty-clackty noise of the Alfa purring away as it stitched.

All finished, I turned the Land Rover towards home and a well needed break.

The sun began to break through the heavy cloud throwing shafts of light through the grey canopy just to remind me that it won't rain forever. I passed near the Cuckmere Valley that had become an inland sea, much as it must have been long ago. Flocks of migrating birds were heading over the cliffs towards the golden coasts of Spain and Africa for an easy winter.

I thought I would stop off at Beachy Head on the way home to soak up the day.

I wound my way along the twisting road climbing up the green downland turf. Up, ever higher. I climbed so high that when I reached the top it looked as if I could see forever.

Beachy Head is a magical place jutting out into the English Channel on a peninsular. Miles of open land, sea and sky that flow before you in a timeless unity.

Sometimes, on special days, if you look hard enough you can see so far that it feels like you can see the future.

Prawning at the base of Beachy Head, a remote spot full of rock pools and teeming with life. On this trip I caught a lobster and several hundred prawns. There is no wilder or more beautiful place on earth.

Eastbourne seafront can look great even when its pouring!

Eastbourne bandstand where the famous band that went down with the Titanic often played. In the distance is the Pier, considered to be the best in Europe.

Living by the sea has always been a great pleasure to me. I often look out to sea at night and see the lights of distant ships far from home.

ENCHANTMENT

Sirens calling, words like thistle down falling,
Upon the sleeping ears of sailors far from home.
Moonbeams dancing, on the tips of waves prancing,
Laying silver paths to the sailors far from home.

Sirens feeling, and their dance so appealing,
Drawing on the hearts of the sailors far from home.
Ship swaying, while the parson's quietly praying,
Praying for the souls of those sailors far from home.

Sirens teasing, smiles on waking lips pleasing,
As the wind whispers to the sailors far from home.
Sun rising, the last chance for their hearts prising,
As the sailors pass by so very far from home.

Alex .I. Askaroff

GHOSTS AND CAT ATTACKS

Dawn was still a while away as I set off up country towards my first call in Maresfield. The relentless commuter traffic was ploughing the highway before me. The red tail-lights of the cars strung out in front of me like carnival lights on a ribbon of tarmac. I hate all the rush-rush driving at this time of the morning. *White-van man* was sitting on my rear bumper trying to get past at any cost. An Alfa Romeo Twin Spark roared past through an impossible gap, disappearing ahead round a bend, shortly followed by white-van man risking his life for a few extra inches of asphalt.

In the UK, statistically, other than teenagers the drivers of white vans are the most dangerous people on our roads. This has caused such a stigma that fewer people buy white vans now. Strange but true.

I was glad when I arrived at my first call.

I parked and headed past a beautiful cottage garden to the corner flat of a large detached house. The house had been split into four flats each named after the four winds – south, north, east and west. I was visiting east wind.

As I entered a curious young tabby tomcat with huge bright eyes surveyed my every move. The cat was not allowed out before 9.30 am when the rush of traffic had calmed a little. He had obviously decided that I was there to amuse him. I kept a careful eye on the moggie. I remembered that a cat had pee'd in my toolbox and that it then attracted the undivided attention of every cat for over a month. It was only after I had scrubbed the box with bleach that they left it alone.

A Toyota machine sat on a poorly-lit table in the corner of the room. It was locked solid.

Trying to turn the beast I asked, "What has happened to this?"

"Oh, I dropped it off the sideboard," she told me in a matter-of-fact you-can-fix-anything voice.

I suddenly remembered the last time I called. She had broken pieces of her machine. She was a policewoman and had asked some of her over-zealous colleagues if they could repair the machine. They sure did fix it – good and proper. Then she called me.

The extra broken parts that they had snapped off with their heavy hands had been kindly left in a bag next to the machine for me. It had taken ages to get the Toyota stitching again.

"Oh you must know what a dozy tart I am by now," she shouted out while washing her hair. "I went to answer the phone and pulled the machine off the table."

Shaking my head I slowly removed the hammer from my tool kit. The one tool I hate to use on a sewing machine. The machine started to move after a few well-placed whacks on the top shaft.

"She lives!" I shouted to Mrs Earl.

At the same time the tabby, no longer able to contain its excitement, ran up my back using me as a pincushion. I squealed like a pig at the butcher's door. I was calling the cat a few names when it decided that because it could not go outside it might as well have a dump under the table where I was working.

As the stench filled the flat I was overcome by the warm smell of yesterday's digested cat food. Then, if things were not bad enough, out marches Mrs Earl. Her head wrapped in a towel turban with Hyacinth deodorising spray in her hand. She attacked the room, with her spray, like a German panzer group moving endlessly forward until the whole room was fumigated.

I sat amongst the mayhem covered in a mist of spray, like early dew. Nevertheless, in true professional style, I kept at the machine. A headache was now upon me, as was the cat that had gone back to crawling up my back!

I escaped with a *thank you dear* ringing in my ears and a gleeful cat staring from between her ankles. As the fresh morning air cleared my muzzy head, I set off for my next call in Nutley. The traffic along the main road had come to a halt near the village. *Probably white-van man smashed into the back of a milk float* I thought.

I turned off the main drag onto a small country lane and escaped the mayhem of modern life. In an instant it was as if I had travelled back in time. The noise, speed and smell left behind on the main road. I knew I was near my next call and made my way through the narrow roads towards her house. I passed two horse-riders dressed in moleskin breeches and Barbour raincoats, one on a lovely chestnut mare and the other on a dapple-grey. They nodded a greeting as I slowly went by.

A watery sun began its daily walk over the Earth, throwing shafts of silvery light into the forest, reflecting off the bare wet branches like a spider's web in the moonlight. Late autumn winds had thrown leaves to the forest floor and laid the vegetation down in blankets of browns and golds.

A large stag well disguised in the woods, chewing on fresh bark, watched me as I passed. His majestic frame supporting large antlers, showing his proud pedigree. He had been ruler of our English forests for thousands of years and he surveyed me with little interest, like a king might a servant, his antlers blending in so perfectly with the branches.

He eyed me more suspiciously as I stopped and took a few pictures. If the stag could talk he would have said, "How dare you interrupt my breakfast! Be off with you, peasant, before I have my manservant give you a good whipping!"

On my way to the next call, goldfinches were busily chasing each other up the lanes, darting from the hedgerows as I drove. Up and down dirt tracks I went, over potholes and through the mud, eventually arriving at her house. I had to demonstrate a new Frister & Rossmann that her husband was buying for her Christmas present.

Within the hour I was off to my next call and she was off to Bluewater Shopping Centre with her friend for a day's *power shopping*. The endless stamina of women and their ability to shop never ceases to amaze me! I have always thought that if the world were really run by men we would still be sitting in caves, eating meat and passing wind.

I arrived at an impressive Georgian house set in grounds with a large pond in front. The private drive led past a field with three horses, their thick winter coats covered from head to foot in mud. Behind the mud, large eyes stared lazily back at me with little passing interest.

As I had called at the vet's house in Ringmer I was greeted at the front door by laughter. "You look just like me on a call," he spouted, a mug of piping hot coffee steaming in his hand.

It looked a welcome sight. His wife was in tears reading a letter from her son, away at boarding school. They were tears of joy as her son had written at his excitement at the coming of Christmas and all the wonderful things that were going to happen.

She read the letter aloud and I was in awe at the grasp the young boy had about the meaning and the love Christmas meant to so many. With two thousand million people on our planet getting ready to celebrate one of the greatest moments in our history this young lad had put into his letter feelings that I had long forgotten. How lucky we are to have the vision, simplicity and clarity of children.

Before long her Brother VX910 was purring along and I was off to my last call of the morning. A haunted house in East Hoathly.

At East Hoathly I found a pretty little cottage built from the ruins of an old chapel. A Riccar professional machine sat on the dining room table waiting for my help. The hook timing had slipped out after Mrs Brough had jammed her grandchild's Christmas pantomime costume in it. Over a cup of tea she told me a ghost story. A true ghost story.

Not long after she moved into the cottage she was sitting in her living room. It was getting dark when she heard a knock behind her. She looked round and a small man with short curly hair and in a long dark coat came out of the cupboard beneath her stairs. He walked casually across the floor in front of her. He came to the wall of the cottage, went straight through and disappeared.

Mrs Brough didn't feel threatened or scared by her uninvited visitor. Being new to the village she wanted to find out who her mysterious visitor was. She invited all the old women of the village for afternoon tea and the matter was discussed thoroughly. A plan was hatched.

They all came together at the village hall with as many old pictures and

documents they could find including all the pictures of villagers that had lived locally. Sure enough amongst the old photographs there he was! A small man in a long dark coat, nicknamed *Foxy*. He had drowned after attempting to walk over the frozen village pond. It was something that he did every winter to check it was safe for the children to play on.

Apparently he had only the one coat and it was far too large for him. Nevertheless he wore it most winters. The story goes that he never had a suit to be buried in and was interred in his coat. Mrs Brough now knew who her visitor was. Although she has been at her cottage for over 20 years he has yet to call again. She never locks the cupboard under the stairs, "Saves him knocking," she told me.

With my work finished for the morning I pointed my trusty beast towards the downs on the distant horizon and headed for home. A well-deserved lunch of beans on toast topped with fried bacon and a cup of tea was waiting for me to demolish.

The hall in the Mermaid Inn in Rye haunted by at least nine ghosts it is a wonderful place to stay. It is in one of the prettiest streets anywhere in the world.

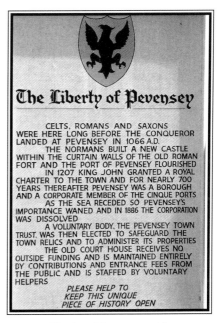

The sign at Pevensey gaol in Pevensey High Street.

Arthur Conan Doyle spent much of his life in Crowborough, East Sussex, a statue of him stands at the High Street crossroads. His grave is down in the New Forest. The simple wording is touching and brilliant – Steel True, Blade Straight.

Sir Arthur Conan Doyle's study at Groombridge Place on the East Sussex border. Conan Doyle lived in Crowborough for 30 years and loved the area. I am sitting at the desk waiting for inspiration. The blank expression shows it did not work!

WATERING THE WOODWORM

A while back I met Mrs Rowland who lives in Bexhill just along the coast. Her husband narrated a tale from his youth. I must say he did it with such flair and enthusiasm that I felt I had re-lived it with him.

When he was 10 his mother was given a very old Singer machine. It was set in a lovely Victorian wooden case. The machine was lavishly inlaid with mother-of-pearl. Now before everybody starts on *Singer never made a machine with mother-of-pearl* his mother still has the machine as proof, though not quite in its original form. You'll see why as you read on.

When the machine arrived home his dad noticed that the wood was riddled with woodworm. As he overheard his parents discussing the problem with a typical child's ingenuity he came up with his own solution!

He waited until his parents were out and struggled upstairs with the machine to his bathroom. In the corner of the bathroom was an old copper tub for boiling water – long gone now in these days of convenience. From the tub he boiled enough water to half-fill the bath and he hoisted the machine, case and all, over the side of the bath and plopped it into the boiling water.

Although it was heavy the machine floated. Stumped for a moment he had a brainwave, rushed downstairs and grabbed his mother's cast-iron smoothing-irons. The old sort that you heated by the fireside before doing the ironing. He placed these around the lid and it slowly sank with a few burps and bubbles. Proud of his ingenious method of drowning the woodworm in a steaming bath he went out to play and, just like a typical ten year-old, forgot all about the machine.

When his parents came home his father went up to the loo. His shouts were heard up the street and everyone came rushing to see what was happening.

The little boy was summoned to the bathroom where the sewing machine case had peeled apart and was floating in layers around a brown filthy bath. He explained that his intentions had been to drown the little monsters.

They all looked on in disbelief and he was duly sent to bed.

He knew he wasn't in too much trouble because he heard his mum and dad roaring with laughter. The next day he scrubbed out the bath and promised to build his mum a new case and many years later he did just that.

The sewing machine is still working fine and except for the handmade case it shows no sign of the trauma it went through all those years ago when a little boy thought he would teach some woodworm how to swim.

Eastbourne seafront at the start of the tourist season.
Eastbourne blends Victorian charm with modern tourism in the perfect mix.
There is something for everyone here.

BILLS'S CHRISTMAS STORY

Bill Prestley was one of those characters I just love to meet. He lives with his wife near Eastbourne in the ancient market town of Hailsham.

A superb Norman church, right in its centre, dominates the town. On clear mornings the early sun catches the gold tops of the four spires and blazes out its holy light to the surrounding villages. The town dates back to Roman times and it still has a market just off the town centre every week. You can buy everything at the market from fresh cheese to a live cow.

Now in his 80s, Bill was a window cleaner in a part of London called the East End. He was born at the outbreak of the Great War in 1914 and he grew up with a London that is very different to the one we have today. Bill's father was also a window cleaner. He cleaned the windows in his local area for over 40 years. Bill's father was a well-known sight around his area with his ladders strapped to a wooden cart that rolled down the cobbled streets of Victorian London.

As soon as Bill left school he joined his dad on the rounds. Times were changing. Horses were making way for cars and the smells of old London also changed. From the smell of horse manure to that of petrol fumes. Bill remembers a unique smell that would hang over London. It would rain after a dry spell and the stench of 50,000 horses and their by-products would hang in the air so thick you could cut it with a knife.

There was an upside to the smell. Most gardens in London had wonderful flowers and vegetables thanks to the horses. On many occasions Bill's window-cleaning buckets would return home full of fresh-steaming horse manure. At the turn of the century there were over 12,000 Hansom cabs working the streets of London. By the thirties there were less than 500.

Between Walworth and Southwark there is a part of London called The Elephant & Castle. It had a horse yard where you could buy a horse 24 hours a day, every day of the year, except on Christmas day.

Bill carried on in his father's footsteps cleaning windows around his area for over five decades. Progressing from a cart to a bicycle, with a bolt-on carriage for his ladders, then to his first car and later to a Sunbeam Talbot that was completely impractical for his work but it looked good as he progressed through his *Jack the Lad* days. Later on he ran, and stuck to using, vans.

Years passed, times changed. The War came and went. The fifties flew by and still old Bill cleaned windows on his rounds. He was well known around his part of the East End. Almost as timeless as old River Thames herself.

Bill would get most of his weekly shopping needs from his customers. Fruit and veg off the barrow boys. Fish, caught locally by Harry from out of the river, that would include lovely sole and his favourite, jellied eels from traps set under Tower Bridge. His meat came from Dewhursts the butchers and his presents, such as Easter eggs and the like, came from his local Woolworths.

The days, weeks and years passed by much the same.

Bill married and settled down, started a family and carried on getting up at 4:30 am every morning to clean windows. He started early but by the time the lazy chimes of Big Ben had struck midday he would be on his way home. He had one break in the morning at Percy's Half Way House, a cafe, where he would pop in for six of drippin', which were six slices of hot toast with fresh beef fat and a mug of tea, a breakfast that he ate every day for 40 years.

By 1964 he had watched dawn break over London for half a century. He had seen a London that had been almost unchanged for centuries become a modern thriving capital. His evening's entertainment would usually be having a smoke outside in the street chatting with neighbours and watching all the kids play footie in the road together.

Later he would be sitting in front of the telly, occasionally getting up to bang it as the black and white lines reverberated up and down whilst trying to watch the end of Dixon of Dock Green, a popular weekly police drama that always ended with Dixon touching his helmet, bending his knees and saying "Evening all" or Steptoe and Son, the hilarious life of two rag 'n' bone men.

Yes, times were changing forever. No more hanging the front door key on a piece of string through the letterbox. No more windows left open while you were out or money in the milk bottle on Thursdays for the milkman. Inevitably crime grew with the City until one Christmas Eve it caught up with Bill.

Christmas Eve started as usual. A quick cuppa then out of the door before five. Off to work. Ladders strapped on the van. The same routine he had done thousands of times before.

This day was not going to be a normal day! It was going to be a day Bill would remember the rest of his life. *Don't worry no one is killed. This is a light-hearted story.*

As Bill went round his local shops cleaning windows he also bought his Christmas goodies. Fresh bread from the baker. A stack of vegetables and fruit, a pot of eels for Boxing Day. Fresh turkey ordered the month before from George at Dewhursts. The present he bought his wife from the local Singer shop was the very latest model from Germany. It was advertised as the finest sewing machine ever made.

A great surprise gift. It was the most expensive Singer in the shop and seemed to do almost anything. When Bill had first seen it demonstrated he was so impressed he jokingly asked if it could *add his month's money up and take it down to the bank for him.*

By 11 am his van was full of everything he and his family needed for a good-old traditional Christmas. He finished off his last job at Woolworths and went back to the van to pack his ladders for the last time and go home for the festivities.

Bill rounded the corner to see or rather not see, his van.

At first he looked at the bare patch of road in a perplexed way, unsure what could have happened. He glared up and down the street. He even walked to the corner to look up the road. His mind working furiously.

Slowly it dawned on him. The van had been stolen!

Dropping the ladders he ran back into Woolworths. Bill told Harry the manager. Harry phoned the Old Plod. They couldn't believe anyone would nick Bill's tatty van. It stuck out like a sore thumb and could be spotted for a mile.

Everyone knew it.

The police put out a major alert. After all this was Bill's van!

Bill ran to all of his customers telling everyone to keep a sharp lookout for the van. He phoned his wife to break the terrible news. He told her the van and all their Christmas treats were gone.

"They hav' bin bleedin' harf-inched!" Bill tells her.

Bill decided the only thing he could do was to wait and make the best of it. He went round and picked up more fruit and vegetables, more bread and beer. Not one of the shops charged him a single penny. He even got another turkey – and on Christmas Eve that was almost impossible.

Luckily George, the butcher, always put a couple by for emergencies. He would reckon on at least one toff coming in to the shop at the last minute to buy a turkey he had forgotten to order. Loaded up with all his replacement goodies Bill struggled home to his wife.

As he turned into his street there, parked outside his house, was his van!

He almost ran to the door where his wife was waiting with the good news. Albert, from the paper shop, on his way home had spotted the van less than two miles away. He had chased a couple of lads down the road but they were too quick for him as they scampered off. He drove the van back to Bill's house.

Bill's wife told him the story. Albert, who was a bit worse for wear after a few early celebration drinks, was embellishing his story to the kids in the lounge.

Set out on the lounge table was everything, all his fruit and veg, his beer. Not one thing had been stolen. The jellied eels, even the turkey was there. The presents were still wrapped.

"Well what am I going to do with this lot then?" asks Bill pointing to his duplicate lot of shopping.

Bill's wife replies, "You can do the same with that as you can with this."

She took Bill by the hand into the kitchen. There on the table was another complete set of Christmas food. Bill's wife had been out as soon as she had heard the news and had bought everything they needed for Christmas too!

That Christmas they had three turkeys, three tins of assorted biscuits, three huge boxes of chocolates and more drink than ever. The kids had so much food that they felt ill but they all had a great time. Everyone in the street had cold turkey for a week and a memory was made to last a lifetime.

When Bill retired, 12 years ago, he and his wife moved down from London. He had worked on the same round that his father had trodden in the 1890s doing the same job until well past retirement age.

Between them they had cleaned some of the same windows for over a century in the East End of London. They had seen everything from Queen Victoria's Silver Jubilee to the Blitz and men walking on the Moon.

I spent ages fixing a small electrical fault on that Singer. The same one Bill had bought that Christmas, all those years ago. I spent even longer listening to stories about life in the East End of London.

It made me very late but I would not have missed it for the world.

These words were written on a cold January morning sitting in my car waiting for my first call.

JANUARY SUNRISE AT BRIGHTLING

I watch as the sun slowly stretches dawn over Brightling.
Shivering brambles clutching yesterdays forgotten fruit
Bow to the unceasing easterly wind. A cold pale sky,
Is casting shaky silhouettes of the bare tipped hedgerows.
Its naked growth stretches skyward to a frozen heaven.
A chilled robin perches upon an empty beer bottle,
Discarded during the heat of a late autumn evening,
That pleasant season now seems like a thousand years ago.
A weak sunrise brings no warmth to this icy daybreak.
The bitter black tarmac has long since forgotten the haze,
That once melted its rigid edges into the green verge.
Those baying hounds which spread their bark across last summer's air,
May never again rise to the call of a huntsman's horn,
Ice bound horseshoe treads leave testament to a stirring chase.
Today even the black scavenger of the countryside,
Goes hungry, as she reluctantly soars over the Weald,
Searching for such scraps that only a crow could survive on.
The Brightling Obelisk casts its longest shadow, westward,
Toward the hamlets of Three Cups Corner and Dallington.
Cattle huddle around Farmer Cox down at Sheepshaw farm,
While he tirelessly lays out the hay through their misty breath.
January, the season where all country life shudders,
And I see this cold sunrise stretching dawn, over Brightling.

Alex.I.Askaroff

MEMORIES

"It ain't stopped rainin' since last bleedin' winter!" our window cleaner declared. Mind you, he should know, his job depends on the weather.

Once he had calmed down with a cup of adrenaline in the disguise of coffee he improved on his statement. "Well it rained most weeks anyways."

Eddie was really good at his job. The outdoor life was for him. He had cleaned not only our house windows but those at the factory and all our family's as well. Looking back on it I think he was probably right. It did feel like a poor summer had passed almost unnoticed.

It was the Waterboard boss's dream. A world of water with towns dotted in between. Each full of people paying ridiculous prices for one of God's greatest gifts. Water is truly *manna from heaven*. Still, I must not get started. It is bad for my blood pressure and dangerous for my dog that hides at the first sign of a brown envelope floating towards the doormat.

The New Year started just as miserably but today, against all scientific prediction, the January sun appeared in an azure-blue sky. There was not a cloud in sight. Perhaps a freak hailstone slung out of the Earth's atmosphere had misaligned one of their weather satellites and they had given us the forecast for outer-Siberia by mistake.

My car was out of action being serviced and I had decided to catch up on a few of the jobs around the house. There was the old Singer 15k that had been waiting patiently for me to replace the broken needle bar, then the overlocker with a chipped looper and the Bernina 801 Electronic with power failure.

When I am busy with house calls these jobs have to wait for my *catch up days,* as I call them. Nevertheless, before I started I wanted to grab a few seconds in the glorious sunshine however cold it might be. Not one to waste such an opportunity, I found a little spot by the shed where the icy wind could not reach me and plonked my rusty folding picnic chair down. Its blue and white stripes groaning at the unaccustomed weight placed upon it.

Some of the whitewashed properties down my road were reflecting the sun almost as if they were rejoicing. I lay back and closed my eyes for a second. The warm sun pouring on to my pale face, which was definitely suffering from some sort of light-deficiency syndrome. I was suddenly whisked away to Southern France. Visions of white villas dotting the green hillside all bathed in the glorious light. A hint of salt in the air summoned an imaginary bay stretching around my scene. The sun sparkling off the sea.

With my head leaning against the warm shed, I imagined the birds singing in the olive groves and almond blossom was drifting aimlessly on the breeze. Rows of lemon trees lined the dusty roads and wild geraniums flowered from every nook and cranny in the open stonewalls.

When I was around 11 a French dressmaker, Madame Compte, whisked me away to France. She spoke no English and I no French. Mumsie had planned it all, however she had failed to inform me. One moment I was eating breakfast at home, the next I was on board a ferry bound for foreign shores!

We stared at each other on the crossing. I was wondering how much my mum would have paid her and for how long was I to be tortured. God only knows what was running through her mind.

We spent around 14 weeks travelling around France. Staying in country villages and towns making dresses and clothes for her clients. We walked for hours in the forests or around the towns. I believe she liked the travelling as much as I did. It was a silent partnership and a very happy one.

We spent a month in Paris with her relatives who regularly swore every time the word *England* was mentioned. After about the third month I was able to understand the conversations but said little. I was a fly on the wall. The French food was adorable and I put on over 20lbs in weight. Having no money for clothes I squeezed into what I had taken with me. I looked like an over-ripe tomato in my red nylon t-shirt.

I loved that summer wandering around Paris, like a lost tourist, and the hazy, dusty days in Fremoville where I would stare out of the window waiting for my dressmaker. Watching the swallows pick insects off the church steeple in the afternoon sun.

One day I saw her returning with the most beautiful chicken in her willow basket. It was clucking away happy as can be. I was delighted that she had brought me a pet, even if it was a chicken. I did not say too much that evening as we sat down to chicken-surprise for dinner!

From then on I would watch out to see what poor animal was coming next. I had a hard time eating the pretty fluffy rabbit – but what a cream sauce she made!

I opened one eye and returned from my childhood holiday. My dog, Rolly, was examining a single, foolhardy crocus that had stuck its yellow head out into the winter sunshine. As the only bit of interest in an otherwise blank garden at least it was something different for her attention. I could tell from her expression that she did not like the taste.

I had a faint and possibly misguided recollection that saffron came from these delicate little beauties and cost more than it's own weight in gold. This thought was wasted on Rolly as she coughed up a slime-ridden petal.

With no warning the sun suddenly disappeared. Gazing skyward I could see a blanket of cloud moving menacingly towards the horizon. The wind found where I was sitting and gave me a cold reminder of whose garden this is in winter.

I folded my chair and headed for the comfort of my radiator indoors and a mug of warm cocoa. My *catch up* day was about to start.

IT COULD ONLY HAPPEN TO ME

Many funny and embarrassing incidents have happened to me on my travels over the years. I will share some of them with you. They are just unconnected incidents that happened during my daily routine. Now you know why I called this book series Random Threads.

Like the first time I called on Mrs Court. She lived miles away from anywhere on a remote farm. Her bungalow was being refurbished so she was living in a mobile home when I visited. It was about 9 am and, as I start at seven most days, I was well into my day.

I walked through the farmyard past the geese that were making a right old racket. Past two rather large bloodhounds, that inspected me menacingly, I knocked on the front door and waited. No answer. I knocked again and checked my watch. I was about half an hour early.

I thought she must be out shopping or dropping the children off at school. Anyway, I decided to hit the road and come back later. I walked away from the mobile home towards my car.

I heard a voice. "Hello. Can I help you?"

I turned to see a woman's head sticking out from behind the door. Her hair all in tangles and her make-up smudged from the night before. Now all this seems quite innocent but you cannot see what I can. The door is frosted glass. The woman is completely naked and is pressed against the glass door.

I am looking straight at her and completely tongue-tied. The frosted glass did nothing to hide her birthday suit. I could only suppose that being half-asleep and not thinking straight she thought the door covered her.

"Er, I have," I stop, trying to concentrate. What have I come here for? Think boy, think! "I have come to do something. Oh yes I have come to fix your washing machine."

"Washing machine? I haven't got a washing machine in here!"

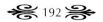

Damn, what am I saying? "Sorry, I mean – you know, the, the – " I look away trying desperately to think straight. "I have come to fix the thingamajig." Ah yes! At last the words arrive. "The sewing machine – that's it! I have come to fix your sewing machine."

"Oh, of course. You are a bit early," she replies, "hang on a second I need to get some clothes on."

There was no need to tell me that lady, no need at all.

Then there was the woman that I called on who never let me in. It was a bright sunny morning and I was in a cheerful, upbeat mood. I rang the bell and waited, whistling away. The door opened and the woman looked on inquiringly. What came out of my stupid mouth?

"Don't worry Madame, it's not the Jehovah's Witnesses, just the sewing machine man."

There was a chilling silence as a look of horror spread across the woman's face. Then the words that still make me shudder.

"Well, you may not be a Jehovah's Witness, but I am!"

The door slammed. Did I feel stupid or what?

Oh yes, what about the sewing machine that had been in the loft for years? I was asked to fix this machine. Everything was going splendidly until I plugged it in.

The woman was upstairs on her way down and she called to me, "Would you like a cup of tea."

Suddenly I was running out of the house with her smoking machine under my arm. Just as I had plugged it in the motor shorted and a flame shot out followed by thick smoke. I grabbed it and rushed for the front door – passing the shocked woman on the way.

"Two sugars please."

Then there was the time that I had dropped in on an upholsterer. He was a right old skinflint, as tight as you could get. He had a small shop that just managed to make a bit of money. He was good at his job but was he tight?

Or what!

I never dropped thread on his floor as he would takes ages picking it up and winding it onto a reel to be used later. He would do this in slow motion in front of me – as a lesson.

Moan! He could moan for England. All the time I was there he would be muttering about having to pay me. He was like a modern version of Scrooge.

Well, one day I was there and he needed to deliver a chair. "Mind the shop will you Alex? I will only be a minute. Any orders you take you can have ten percent!"

He laughed, a hand-rolled cigarette stuck in the corner of his unshaven face, and departed.

No sooner did he leave than the manager of Eastbourne's largest hotel walked in. He wanted all his settees re-covered for the new season. I ran through a few fabrics with him and we arrived at a rough estimate of £10,000. I took all the details and told him we would be in contact shortly. When Jim returned I broke the news that he owed me about £1000 for my few minutes work. Needless to say I never saw a penny of it but I had a laugh, making him stutter and blabber. It was the only time that he ever paid cash to fix his sewing machine.

Anything to get me out of his shop quicker!

I once visited a woman in the middle of her son's birthday party. She had completely forgotten she had booked the appointment. "You might as well come into the madhouse," she shouted over the screaming children. "It can't get any worse than it is already," she said as she dragged the machine out from under the stairs.

As I fixed the machine the kids became transfixed by my work. In the end they were circled around me like a pack of Red Indians around the cavalry.

"You are a clever man," one little girl said to me pulling her curly-red hair out of her mouth.

"Yes, you are," said another with cream and jam all over his face.

Then the magician arrived. Great! I thought, at least I will have some peace and quiet now.

How wrong I was. The magician had seven kids watching him, I had 23!

When I finished and had stitched a nice straight line of sewing along the edge of a tablecloth the children all clapped and cheered. "I could have saved £60 if I had known. I would not have booked the magician!" the woman chipped in over the heads of the staring kids.

That is the best audience I have ever had.

Well now – how about this for embarrassing? I visited a lovely house with a beautiful, large Weimaraner dog. She was very attentive and sat by me as I was fixing her master's machine. I occasionally stroked her as I was working. I thought nothing of it.

That was until I arrived at my next call. Here lived a young Alsatian owned by an old couple. No sooner did I start to work on the sewing machine than the dog started making amorous advances towards me.

The owners could not understand it. Believe me, I was not too happy about it either! This was a big, powerful, young dog with a one-track mind. The owners were trying in vain to drag the amorous, dribbling, beast off me. I was telling it I was married and trying to prove it with pictures of my children.

Nothing would slow him down.

Eventually they managed to get a lead around his neck and between them they dragged the lusting dog into the next room. As I fixed the machine he howled away in the adjoining room in his sweetest, most-appealing, doggy voice. Apparently the dog at the previous house was on heat. The Alsatian had taken one sniff and thought I was his treat for the day.

Talk about a blind date. Boy was I glad to get out of that place.

Over the years dogs have attacked me on several occasions. I once made the owner of a vicious poodle bandage me up before I would repair her machine. However, considering the thousands of calls I make, I have had little problem with dogs. The worst or scariest was when I was called to a huge mansion up a long twisting gravel drive. The front door was painted over and the mansion looked in a poor state. I knew that the front door could not be the one that the owners used and I walked around to the back of the house. I found the back door and knocked loudly.

Nothing happened. I knocked again.

Then, to my horror, I heard the sound of two large dogs howling.

I heard them on the gravel. They were running at full speed from the other side of the house. Nowhere to run! Nowhere to hide!

I put my toolbox down, looked at the ground and braced myself. As the two Doberman came round the side of the house one of them slipped on the gravel and slewed across the drive before recovering. Then running again both ran full-speed at me. A more ferocious sight was hard to imagine.

Images raced through my brain of being tossed like a rag doll. The dogs ran towards me howling like possessed demons with the intent of feasting on my liver. At the last second they stopped running. They were travelling at such a speed that the dog in the lead slid straight into me and knocked me over.

Then they turned and ran off. I had survived unscathed, almost.

The owner told me they did that to everyone, "They like to have their fun," he said. It would have been nice to tell me before my heart attack. Luckily I was not upset and did not give him any verbal, he turned out to be a Lord.

Sewing is something that rises above class. It is something that is very special in this respect and most unusual. People sew for need, pleasure, a hobby and a living. In the same day I had visited three manor houses – a Lord, a Right Honourable and a Lady, then visited a sheltered home where I thought I was going to be mugged.

I have been to areas where I was lucky not to lose my car's wheels and I have been in houses with enough marble on the floor to make headstones for a large cemetery. One minute I might be in stables fixing a rug machine, the next in a factory.

I once attended a Woman's Institute meeting where 40 women made more noise than a screaming mob at a pop concert. It was supposed to be a *Knit*

& *Nat* but I did not see anyone knitting. How anyone heard anything amazed me. I fixed one machine that a woman had brought with her to the meeting then spent two hours giving an impromptu lecture on the birth of the sewing machine industry.

The hall went from complete mayhem to silence as I rambled on about Thomas Saint, James Gibb, Elias Howe, Isaac Singer and Charles Raymond. It had all started when one woman asked me who actually invented the first decent sewing machine.

It is one of the great pleasures of my job that I meet every type of person God put on this earth. From old war heroes to new mothers.

It is not always good news. You meet the cheats as well. Like the tailor that called me out, got me to repair his machine, bought loads of extra feet and bobbins and needles and wrote me a cheque. I got home to find a message from his bank saying that he had cancelled his cheque. It turned out this was a trick of his. You could either take him to court or let it go.

Most people let it go, so did I.

It backfired on him when no one would fix his machine and he went out of business. He offered to pay me cash, any amount, when he was desperate but on principle I told him no. I still get a few bounced cheques every year. To this day I could not predict who will bounce a cheque. I work on the principle of trusting everybody until they cheat. Luckily the percentage is so low that it is always to my advantage.

There was one particularly nasty person who tricked me. She turned up late on a Friday afternoon and bought a brand new machine, all sweetness and roses. She paid me by cheque and took the machine away.

Monday morning at nine sharp two big thugs appeared with the new machine. "This is not what my mum wants, she wants her cheque back, now!"

I was in no position to argue. I handed them the cheque and took the machine. Later that day I checked the machine out and found it full of fluff. I found out later that she had made all the new curtains for her house in a weekend and that was the only sewing she would do for a few years. Some time before she had pulled exactly the same trick on a colleague.

It is not always me that gets the short end of the stick. I came across an aircraft engineer that had taken his wife's machine apart. His wife had told him to leave it alone but, being an engineer of the highest standard, he decided that such a simple machine could not possibly beat him.

I turned up and found 32 pieces of the machine all neatly laid out on a large table. Each piece had a bit of string on it and a card explaining where it had come from. I told him straight away that it would take hours to put it back together and I just did not have the time to do it. He begged me, actually begged me on his knees, to fix the machine before his wife got home.

Boy was he scared of her!

I fixed it all and he gave me a huge tip. There was a look of deep gratitude on his face as I left. I think I had saved him from a severe beating. As I left he made me promise not to admit that I had been to his house.

Much the same thing happened when I met an organ tuner who had taken his mother's machine apart. I fixed it and he gave me a tip on the understanding that I never tell his mother that he had had to call me out.

My biggest surprise of all came when I called on a very old dear. I had just started calling on customers and every penny I earned was desperately needed. She was partially deaf, only had one eye and needed a good shave. She took me up into her spare room and introduced me to her 1932 Singer 66k. She had bought the machine new, it was fine but the motor had stopped.

It was not the normal motor but a semi-industrial one slung beneath the table. I said to her that I would not be able to fix it. "What did you say?" she shouted back.

"I will not be able to fix your motor."

She said, "Thank you," walked out of the room and closed the door.

I scratched my head. What was I supposed to do now? She must have misunderstood me. I looked once more at the motor. I had never seen anything like it but I thought *I am stuck here so I might as well have a go.*

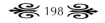

Well the time passed and I got deeper and deeper into the motor. Then, right in the middle of the windings I spied a broken wire. I could not believe it! Such a simple defect to repair and so obvious. I soldered the wire and slowly rebuilt the motor. I had been in the house over two hours but the machine was working beautifully.

I called the lady. Then I shouted for her and then I went to find her. Eventually I found her and, through a mixture of shouting and sign language, managed to convey to her that I had fixed her machine. She was delighted.

Then I had to break the news to her how much she owed me. At that time it would normally come to £15 but I had been there much longer than normal and had used a few parts. However I thought that I would charge her the same anyway. I had the feeling that £15 was going to be an awful lot of money to her.

I told her how much she had to pay me and she went off to get the cash. She came back and put £120 in my hand. I shouted to her that she had given me over £100 too much. She got my hand and folded it around the money and said, "I know how to count young man. You deserve every penny my dear, you've made an old woman very happy."

I had just the opposite call the next day. I came across an old sailor, *a salty sea dog,* as he described himself. He spun me a few yarns of his old days and made me a cup of tea so strong that the spoon could stand up in it. I spent ages fixing his old machine and when I was finished he pushed a five-pound note into my hand and slapped me on the back.

"I hope that covers the cost me old matey," he winked at me.

I looked at the money and looked at the white-haired old sailor, "That will be fine sir," I replied.

As I drove away he was standing in the door of his home, a pipe stuffed in the side of his mouth. *Talk about Popeye the Sailor Man* I thought. Above the doorway was a sign, The Captain's Bunk. He waved to me as I went and smiled.

The smile gave it away. The old dog knew exactly what he was doing! I

could just see him down in the Mess onboard his old ship. A few of his chums around the card table all bluffing their wages away. He had caught me fair and square.

The most embarrassing call of all, it could only happen to me, was when I called in to a customer that I had been to for many years. As I was working away we were chatting. She happened to mention that her husband had left her. Now, I remembered her hubby – each time I called he just sat in the chair opposite me and took the mickey out of me.

To make her feel a little better about her horrible husband running away, probably with another woman half his age, I consoled her by saying in a bright bubbly voice, "Well he was a lazy sod anyway. You are better off without him."

"No Alex," she says, "he didn't leave like you think. He died!"

Now that is what I call putting your foot in it. Big time!

I wanted the ground to open up and swallow me whole. Luckily she knows me and realised I would never have said anything like that if I had known so I got away with a real humdinger. I still blush when I think of it.

It is not always me that puts my foot in it. I called, awhile back, on a young woman who was in a foul mood. What had happened was that she had woken late and shook her husband. "Wake up Steve, you'll be late, Steve wake up." Her husband's name was Jeff!

What about the time I called on Mrs Jackson. She was a complete stranger and had got my number from the phone directory. I called at her house, just around the corner from me and fixed her machine. Everything was fine when I left. Next day the phone rings and it is Mrs Jackson. "My machine was working beautifully but the belt has snapped. Could you pop in and put a new one on?"

"OK, I'll be round in a second."

I jumped into my car, whipped around the block and knocked on the door. Mrs Jackson opens the door. I knew the machine was in the kitchen as I had only fixed it yesterday.

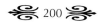

"Hello, I know where it is," I said and brushed past her with my tool kit and the new belt. I got into the kitchen – no machine. I looked around as she came in behind me and asked, "Where is the machine then?"

"I put it in the bedroom where it lives," said Mrs Jackson in a most perplexed way.

"Do you want me to pop upstairs and do it then?"

"Do what?" she asked in a worried tone.

"Fix the machine."

"But you did that yesterday," she said in a now frightened voice.

"I know but I have brought the belt."

"Belt?"

"Yes," I said, thinking her a bit odd. She had only put the phone down on me two minutes ago.

"Why would I want a belt?" She asked, now in a bit of a state.

"You did ring me just now?"

"No!"

"Are you sure?" Stupid question really but by now neither of us had got a clue as to what is going on. "Oh, I'd better go then."

"Yes that would be nice." I can see a sense of relief on her face as I left. I walked out the door and heard the locks clank, clank behind me.

I rushed home, my head spinning. What was going on? I went through my calls from the previous day. Bold as day there were, in fact, two Mrs Jacksons on my list! Now it all made sense. I had called on the wrong one!

Incredibly embarrassed I phoned her immediately to explain the mistake. She listened politely but said little.

Some time later I saw her coming towards me in our shopping centre. She put her head down and walked over to the other side of the parade. I know

she thinks I am mad.

Then there were the two men, of slightly different persuasion, that were so pleased to see me. I was greeted by a shocking-pink silk dressing gown with an over-ripe-plump, middle-aged, man inside it. "Oh do come in young man – Bert!" he called out down the corridor, "there is a nice young man at the door. He has come to see about your machine."

Once in the lavishly-painted bungalow, that looked more suited to a brothel, I was ushered about like a boy arriving at the Turkish Baths. They were so excited, almost fit to burst.

"Ooh, Charlie, hasn't he got nice eyes?" Bert said wafting around examining me with his expert eye. Bert's dressing gown was just brushing against my arm as he giggled past, his hair wrapped in a towel like Carmen Miranda. If you saw the two walking down a street, in normal clothes, they would look more like hairy coal-miners than two fancies.

"Don't bend over in front of Charlie, it gives him a headache," Bert spouts, waving a hand limply around as if it was not joined to his arm.

"Keep your back to the wall with that bitch!" Charlie scratches back at his partner in his sourest manner, wiggling off to the kitchen for a drink from a pot that was covered with a knitted multicoloured tea-cosy.

I fixed their Jones sewing machine at the speed of light while the two flapped around me like a couple of overweight peacocks. Once done, I made quickly for the door. Two menacing men close at my rear followed me up the hall. Bert leant forward and pinched my bum and giggled.

"Now Bert control yourself," said Charlie smacking Bert's hand playfully.

"What a nice man," said Bert, blinking his eyelashes at me.

"Oh yes, a very nice man," chipped in Charlie.

"Yes, a very, very, nice man!" retorts Bert.

"Come back and see us soon!" they both shouted as they waved me off.

"Don't be a stranger now," Charlie calls out to me.

"Missing you already," Bert adds, followed by a kiss blown in my direction.

Laughing, they put their arms around each other and wiggled inside. I think they had had their fun for the day, scaring me to death. I stalled my car twice trying to pull away. Not that I was shaken – much!

Rolly, our family pet and troublemaker.
The Patterdale is a highly intelligent farming dog,
bred for keeping the farm free of pests.

Beachy Head and lighthouse, built at the turn of the century.
As a child I had always fancied being a lighthouse keeper. Of course now they are all automated but
I remember well the post being delivered from long cables that once stretched to the cliffs.

TO BARTER OR NOT TO BARTER

Over the years and the many thousands of customers that I have called on it is little surprise that occasionally I have taken items instead of money. I have little doubt that if money were to disappear I would be able to survive quite happily with a barter system from olden days.

More than once I have returned home with goods in exchange for services and had Yana give me the look before lifting her head in despair. Most of the items were of little monetary value but to me they were most welcome. Below are listed a few of the weird and wonderful items that have travelled home with me.

My son's first Guitar, that put a smile on the boy's face.

Dozens of old, mostly useless sewing machines but there was once a Victorian Bradbury that I still have, a white 221k and a pristine Featherweight that would have made scrooge smile.

Two pinnies and three aprons.

Endless jars of homemade jam and marmalade in January.

Cakes, oh yes, what cakes over the years. All my surplus weight could be put down to Sussex folk and their baking from the Womens Institute to country fayres, all are great excuses for me. The one cake that I could never forget was a carrot and raisin cake with a cream cheese frosting. Diana Betts who made the cake is the only *Sussex Sewing Machines lifetime honorary member*. When I repair her machines, as I won't take money she lavishes me with goodies.

One other food item I remember so well was a real Italian Pizza. Tina who grew up in a poor part of Naples made it. The original pizzas were food for the workingman. Thick and filling with a topping that would have made Emperor Nero announce a public holiday. A mixture of tomatoes, garlic, anchovies and spices all soaked in virgin olive oil. The amazing thing was it had no cheese. After feasting on it I had to lie down for an hour, what a pizza.

A huge slab of walnut and another of ash for woodturning from a wheelwright near Hooe.

Plants of all sizes and colours for the garden. Our garden is more of a trip down memory lane than a garden.

A concrete pattern mould! Don't ask I still have no idea why I got it either.

A shrimp net, great swap that, I still use it.

Walking sticks. Yes, walking sticks so far I have accumulated about a dozen from all over my area. No I have not pinched them from poor old dears who cannot struggle to the shops without them. Most are the ornamental type made in local woods.

Eggs, loads and loads of eggs. If a farm has eggs I always come home with some and duck eggs are my favourite.

Fish. I have arrived home with everything from jellied eels to smoked salmon, slabs of cod and dressed crab. If I bump into a fishmonger's wife I am onto a winner.

Oil cans. Yes, I have a soft spot for sewing machine oil cans and have around 50 so far in a multitude of designs.

Hand knitted jumpers. Always a bit tricky that one. Once I am cornered it is hard to say no to some old dear that has spent a month knitting the most atrocious multi-coloured monster.

Five whisky tumblers. I still have no idea why she gave them to me!

A bag of elastic bands from a postman.

An old cricket bat from an old cricketer. It was full of woodworm and went on the bonfire, probably worth a fortune today.

Sewing machine attachments. If I had a pound for every person that pulled out a box of attachments for an old machine I would be wealthy. I must have 1000 or more in boxes all over the place.

A small, barley twist oak table. That was a great deal.

Amongst the huge number of food items from cabbages to cream the one item I remember for its outstanding taste was a slab of slow-dry-cured bacon from a pig farm. I have still never tasted bacon as good.

A brace of pheasants from a poacher. They were great except I nearly broke a tooth on a pellet.

Books, several books and a few pictures along the way from local artists.

Compost, life just would not be the same without a few nice bags of horse manure and compost for the roses.

Many tools including a depth gauge for my lathe from the drawer of a woman who had kept it for over 20 years with no idea what it was. My favourite of all was a huge Record vice from a coffin makers workshop that held the coffins in the workshop. If I ever get around to it I am going to make my coffin with the help of that vice.

Finally, saving the best till last. Of all the things I have brought home, countless times were the wonderful stories from the people I have met over the years. They are simply priceless.

Croquet at Saffrons. What a way to spend a lazy afternoon.

HOUND DOG

On my travels I often meet some unusual customers. Well, this day was no different.

My first customer ran a Curry restaurant in Seaford some 11 miles up the coast from Eastbourne. I spent an hour fixing a terrible Jones machine that really needed to be run over by a dump truck and used as ballast in a boat. By the time I left I stank like a Bombay brothel and I was yearning for a curry.

My next customer had worked as a pathologist and when he retired from cutting up bodies he worked for an undertaker. A natural progression I suppose. Well now, this young man of 80 years is close to a genius. He repairs everything and every stitch he was standing in was his own work. This bloke was unbelievable. He took me into his sewing room where he was making some new covers for his settee on an ancient Singer 29k bootpatcher. I said to him that it was quite old and he laughed.

Next thing I know I am standing in his garage next to a 200-year-old pole lathe that he converted, via a Ford transmission, into a perfect working metal lathe. On this lathe he had been making bits for his Singer.

Back in his sewing room I noticed a funny table set into the floor. I asked him what it was. You are going to love this boys and girls!

He moved around and started unscrewing a handle on the side. Lo and behold up from the floor rises the table. Fully adjustable to any height. It is where he cuts out all his fabrics and, when it is no longer needed, it sinks back into the floor.

My eyes nearly popped out of my head. What a great idea! He could sell millions to small workshops all over the world. I asked him where he got it. I should not have! It turned out to be one of his mortuary tables that he had taken from his old job. They used to lay out the bodies on it and lift them to the perfect height to do autopsies, nasty.

For payment I took some spondoronies and a wood-vice that used to hold the planks of coffinwood for smoothing and varnishing.

I shuddered and hit the road thinking about all the different goods that I had taken over the years instead of money. My next call was at a factory to a super-fast twin-needle machine. The machine ran perfectly while cold but as the temperature rose one of the hooks started to seize. Two other engineers had spent weeks looking at the machine but could not figure it out. It took me less than a minute to figure out the problem but another hour to take the hooks apart and reset them so that they would not seize under constant use.

As I was working away I had to keep apologising for the smell of curry that was clinging to my clothes and I was getting a few sarcastic remarks from the machinists.

One of the great parts of my job, as I have often said, is that I am like a fly on the wall. I come into people's daily lives and for a few moments I see everything. Who is flirting with whom, who is in a temper, whose birthday is coming up – all the gossip. I love it!

No sooner have I landed and absorbed all the factory life than I am off. Up and away to my next victim – oops customer!

My favourite part of the morning was in the factory. Dozens of people all working away as they do every day. All at their different stations. The machinists' heads down work buzzing through the machines. The cutters slicing fabric. The packers packing and checkers checking. All busy. Then the boss whipped through at the speed of light, running here and there like a headless chicken.

Do chickens really run around without their heads?

On the radio Elvis Presley came on. He was singing *You ain't nothing but a hound dog*. Within seconds every person in the room was singing, tapping their feet, twisting and turning. Before long the whole factory was resounding to a poor karaoke version of Elvis. It was brilliant!

The song finished and everyone just carried on working as if nothing had happened. It was fantastic. I was a silent observer watching Elvis work his magic on the crowd and no one had the slightest clue.

People ask what makes a person great. Well, that morning I saw.

After my call at the factory I made my way up to my next call in Broad Oak near Heathfield. Broad Oak is a small rural town steeped in history. This part of East Sussex is well wooded and many ancient stories abound.

Before Christianity swept through our shores the ancient Celtic Druids held power over the common people. Their simple beliefs still survive today. Locals say the word Druid comes from a mixture of two old words. The forests were held in high esteem and no tree was held higher than the great oak. The Druids are said to have taken their name from the ancient name of the great oak and that of a wise man. Oak-wise in old English became Druid. Just local gossip mind and I bet in France they have another story all together, but many a tale holds an acorn of truth.

I drove past nearby Oak Hall, that was once the property of the millionaire tycoon Sir Harry Oakes. George VI knighted Sir Harry in 1939 at his grand home, he held a lavish party to celebrate. Harry's wealth was huge and he had many houses. Legend has it that Harry hid millions of pounds worth of gold in each of his houses around the world in case he needed it in a hurry. Remember it was not long after the Wall Street crash in 1929 and any businessman that could, placed their money in gold.

In 1943 Harry met a gruesome death at his home in the Bahamas. To this day no one has found out who killed him or why. It remains one of the great-unsolved, murder mysteries of our country.

Harry's sudden and brutal death sparked rumours about his stashes of gold, but however much Oak Hall was searched no one has ever found the treasure. Some say that his hoard of gold is still hidden somewhere at Oak Hall just waiting to be found.

How about that for a tempting reason to buy a shovel and go digging! Maybe it is behind a secret panel in the library or under the old Roman remains in the garden?

Before too long I had finished my call and headed up-country into Ashdown Forest, to a small cottage hidden down a winding track amongst the wild bracken and gorse. I was expecting to find an old machine but came face to face with the latest Janome computer that looked like it could whisk you up a couple of eggs while you were sewing on it. Luckily the

machine had a simple fault otherwise it would have been a nightmare.

The morning had disappeared and my belly was calling out for sustenance. I glanced at my watch. It was just after 2 pm. I knew in an instant where to go for lunch. The Duddleswell Tea Rooms. In the forest is the most perfect little English tearooms that serve up cream teas, lunchtime snacks and cakes that make you forget all about calorie counting. They also have one particular food that makes me go weak at the knees, Weald Pie.

Weald Pie is a local pie from this area of the Sussex Weald. It is a mixture in layers, of chicken, ham and pork all laced with apricots set in aspic jelly and baked in heavenly pastry.

I pulled up outside the tearooms and checked my watch, 2.20. I knew that they stopped serving lunch at two so I would have a struggle getting my pie. Remembering Elvis earlier in the day at the counter I put on my best *hound-dog* look and asked for the pie.

"We stop serving at two pm young man."

"Oh, I know! But I am a weary traveller in need of sustenance. Please, pretty please?"

She weakened, smiled and cut me a huge slab of pie. I sat and enjoyed their wonderful fare, washed down with two cups of tea.

I sat watching the other visitors as I scoffed my lunch with a satisfied smile on my face. Many were tourists come to taste the famous Duddleswell afternoon cream-teas, consisting of two lovely fruity homemade scones with a pot of butter, a pot of strawberry jam and a pot of clotted cream. This is all delivered to the table with a pot of tea. One couple, sitting behind me, were constantly squabbling but only in the most amiable way. As they went to leave they paid at the till and moved to the door.

The man opened the door and said, "Muck before the shovel dear."

Laughing she pushed the old fella out of the door in front of her with the quip, "Age before beauty, love, age before beauty!"

I smiled with the girl behind the counter, paid my bill, thanked her once again for the super pie and left.

I drove through the open forest with my funeral parlours vice rattling in the boot. Ashdown Forest has infinite beautiful colours, and miles of open scrub, that roll in undulating hills and forests for miles into the heart of East Sussex. It is here that Henry and his entourage would have hunted deer. Chasing them wildly across the heathland and through the forests before retiring to Bolebrook Castle for venison, roasted over an open fire and jugs of ale.

Ah what it would be like to be a king I thought as I drove, rubbing my full belly with delight. *Then, on the other hand, who could have had such a day as mine? No king that's for sure.*

HERE STOOD
THE OAK TREE,
ON WHICH AN ARROW
SHOT BY
Sir WALTER TYRRELL
AT A STAG,
GLANCED AND STRUCK
KING WILLIAM
THE SECOND,
SURNAMED RUFUS,
ON THE BREAST,
OF WHICH HE
INSTANTLY DIED,
ON THE SECOND
DAY OF AUGUST,
ANNO 1100.

I love this notice in the New Forest. It was William the Conqueror that created the New Forest for his sport, much to the annoyance of the villagers that were moved. If it was an accident! It has to be one of the biggest clangers of all time.

NEW DAWN NEW DAY

The door opened. Standing before me was a pretty woman of about 30 soaking wet and wrapped tightly in a cream towel and as red as a lobster pulled fresh from the fishmongers boiling pot.

"I have come to fix the machine." I announced with a cheerful smile. Being greeted first thing in the morning with such a pleasant sight would make most men smile.

"I am so sorry I was rushing to be ready for you." She said ushering me into her home. "The machine is upstairs I will be with you in a moment."

It was my first call of the morning and I had to be out of her home by 8.30 as she left for work. The machine had ground to a halt altering her sisters wedding dress. She was on the final seem when a loud crunch announced the end of her sewing. I found the problem quickly and got down to business. I was smiling to myself when the woman appeared hair dried, makeup on, and smartly dressed in a light grey trouser suit.

"There that's better." She said putting the finishing touches to her lipstick in front of her mirror. "Now how is my little darling?"

"Just fine," I said. "And the machine is Ok as well."

"Very funny."

I laughed. " I am sure you will be able to finish off your sisters dress with no more problems."

"I won that machine in a *Round The Bay Race* in New Zealand. I never actually won the women's race but after the finish, a man came along and gave me the Pfaff. I was a little bemused, but was not going to hand it back without a fight, so I hightailed it out of there pretty quick."

As I left I could not help remembering all the times I had called to find women and the odd man in towels. Starting at daybreak and up with the larks always brings new adventures. *Never a dull moment* I thought as I

drove to my next customer.

As I followed the morning traffic I could not help thinking how everyone had a story. It does not matter who it was they could probably tell you something fascinating. I decided that when the opportunity arose I would put my theory to the test.

"Where on earth did you find this beauty?" I asked, green with envy. I was looking at a superb 1880's Bradbury treadle machine.

"I bought it out of the Friday Ad. Is it valuable?"

"Not much," I laughed. "I reckon about £400. How much did you get it for?"

"£25, I had no idea it was so valuable will it work?"

"With my magic touch I am sure it will be sewing in no time at all. All we need is a belt and a couple of minor parts. I'll get them from the car."

"Lovely, and I shall put the kettle on, coffee or tea Alex?"

"Coffee with two sugars please." I shouted as I went out the door.

What a buy I was thinking. *Why is it always someone else that finds these treasures!*

Within the hour I was refreshed with coffee and had some basic rules on playing Bridge thrown in to the conversation, which mostly went over my head. I gave the woman a lesson on her Victorian treadle machine that would have been made when *Jack the Ripper* stalked the back streets of London, and headed for my next call.

The morning wore on and my last call was a sad one. I was calling on Mrs Clarence to pick up her sewing machine. I had sold it to her many years before, but now time had taken its toll and she could no longer sew.

"Morning gorgeous." I said as she pulled the door open.

"Oh Alex you do make me smile, come in, come in. Because you have looked after me so well over these last few years I want you to take the machine. I do not want any money for it. It is my way of saying thank you for all your hard work over the years. I wish I could carry on sewing but

my time has come. At 95 I suppose I had to give up eventually. 87 years I have been sewing, a whole lifetime. I started sewing back during the Great War, just little things to help mother and never stopped. I wonder how many reels of thread I have used, if you joined them all up they would probably go around the world. Still, all things come to an end and since Arthur passed on and my hands have gone it is time to stop."

In the following silence, a sadness came over the room as real as if someone had just walked in. I hate it when that happens, a melancholy mood can set in and destroy a fine day as sure as an unwanted rainstorm.

"You can always do a bit of hand stitching." I said trying to break the awkward silence. She held up one of her hands, crippled with arthritis. "Not me Alex, Not me."

I sighed. There was just no way out of this depressing situation, no hope, no light at the end of her tunnel. Her radiance was fading as sure as the end of the day. She had accepted that at 95 she was running out of time and with her failing health and the loss of her fingers there was little more to do than just wait for God.

She seemed like a lonely old girl, left in her home, listening to the clock tick away her remaining life. I had to get out of there as I felt her pain, and it was sweeping over me. I had racked my brains for something that she could do, croquet, bowls, cards, knitting, anything to help her enjoy her last days but I was defeated, my usual cheerful persona had deserted me.

I moved to the door with the machine, knowing that I would never see her again. Knowing that there would be no more calls to service her machine, no more chats over coffee of her younger years.

By the time I was out of the house I felt a lump in my throat, it was just a miserable situation.

"Thank you for coming Alex, it was nice to see you once again. Find a good home for the machine it has been a fine companion over the years. Now Alex, you have a good life and one day when you are sitting alone in a quiet moment, remember me." She smiled sweetly and closed the door. I moved slowly up her little path. As I got to her gate I was feeling totally miserable

the weight of the machine was like lead. I heard the door open behind me.

"Alex," Mrs Clarence called up the path. "Have you got Sky?"

"Yes."

"I have just had it installed, isn't it brilliant! I stayed up all night on Friday. First time for 50 years. You know they show some things that make me blush at 95 and tonight they have Men & Motors from ten. I have set my alarm for it just in case I have a nap. I haven't had so much fun for years."

I laughed. *The old girl had some spirit left in her yet* I thought. My mood lifted and I smiled as I went. Suddenly the machine was as light as a feather. The grim reaper was going to have more trouble than he bargained for trying to drag Mrs Clarence off this planet.

By the time I arrived home I was upbeat, laughing at the thought of what Mrs Clarence was up to each night, with her remote control overheating, as she constantly switched channels. Eddie, our window cleaner had just arrived. Time to test my theory I thought.

"Eddie, would you have a story about anything to do with sewing?"

Eddie looked at me in his usual way, knowing after all these years that I was a borderline nut case at the best of times.

"Actually it so happens that I have. That has surprised you hasn't it! When I was a young man in my prime I had my suits made at Burtons the tailors. I would spend hours choosing from their rolls of cloth, then being measured. A suit would cost me twenty pounds or so, a bloody fortune in 1960. I would pay it off at ten bob a week. It would take me months to pay but when you are a lad that is all we worked for, to look good and have fun. I usually had two or three fittings, just to get it skin tight. I doubt if I would fit into one now, but I had to look the part didn't I!"

"When I picked up the suit it was a big day, and I would wear it down to Clarkes and buy a pair of *winkle pickers* at least three inches longer than the shoes we wear today, and with a point sharp enough to take your eye out. I would get a pair that matched perfectly, then go out for a night on the town, and chat the girls up. I looked like a million quid, those were the days mate."

With that, Eddie swung his ladder around onto the first window and got stuck into his routine. "No time to stop now Alex, you just bring me a cup of coffee before I change my mind and go home. Oh and a slice of Yana's cake would be good."

"How do you know Yana's made a cake?" I asked quizzically as he had only just arrived moments before me.

"With her cooking you can smell it a mile away, now get a move on boy, I haven't got all day."

I left Eddie cleaning windows and went to investigate just what cakes Yana had been baking, with the satisfied knowledge that my theory was proving correct. Another morning had shot by, with the usual mixture of events in my never-ending travels. As I entered my house the warm homely smell of baking wrapped itself around me, and dragged me enthusiastically into the dining room.

What a trial and what a joy these last few years had been. All my hopes had come true as I chased a dream. A dream of a better life. When I had first started my travels and money was so tight I spent most days wondering if I had made the right decision. One day I bumped into the sweetest old dear. While fixing her machine I had told the story of how I started my business. She listened over a cup of tea and then told me something I shall never forget. She told me about happiness.

Happiness is like a butterfly, the harder you chase it the further away it always seems. But, if you wait patiently, one day, you may just find it sitting on your shoulder.

How right she was.

THE END

GLOSSARY

Amish	Followers of Jacob Ammann
Anderson shelter	A backyard bomb shelter
Barrow boys	Market traders
Bite the Dust	To Die
Bounced cheque	Returned by the bank due to insufficient funds
Boot	Car boot – trunk
Booty	Valuable items
Boozer	Public House (Pub)
Bungalow	Single storey building
Chumping	Eating with speed
Conkers	Horse Chestnuts
Cuppa	Cup of Tea
Deck chair	Folding chair. Wooden frame with cloth seat.
Demob	Demobilisation after the war
Doodlebug	German Rocket Bomb
Duvet	Quilt
Earls Court	Exhibition centre in London
Fag	Cigarette
Fiver	Five English Pounds
Folly	A monument often extravagant, unusual or foolish
Frock	Dress
Fry-up	Bacon, eggs, sausages mushroom, tomatoes etc
Grockle	Holidaymaker
Half-a-crown	Old coinage, worth 12.5 pence today
Ham-fisted	Awkward
Hanson cabs	Two wheeled horse drawn carriage
Harrods	A prestige department store in London
Heinz 57	Mongrel Cross Breed
Hostelry	Pub and eating house
Hubby	Husband
Hun	German Soldier
MP	Member of Parliament
Lapsy	Lazy
Lav	Toilet
Lavvy	Toilet
Lay-by	A part of the road where vehicles can stop out of the main stream of traffic
Loo	Toilet
Mary Quant	A 1960s designer
MI5	Military Intelligence section 5
Mobile	Cell phone
MOD	Ministry of Defence
Moggie	Cat

Never-never	Hire purchase
Palaver	Fuss
Pinnie	Apron
Plod	Policeman
Poodled	Go slowly
Pop-His-Clogs	To Die
Posh	Elegant
Plunder	Stolen goods
Pushing up The Daisies	Dead and Buried
Quid	One English Pound
Rag and Boneman	Junk dealer
Road tax	A government tax to allow vehicles on the road
Salems Lot	A film based on a Stephen King novel
Scallywag	Child up to no Good
Sixpence	An old, small coin
Skin-Flint	Tight with Money
Skip	Rubbish Container
Slobbering	To Dribble
Slunk	Creeping in
Smitten	Fallen for Someone
Snuck	Crept Along
Swig	A mouthful of drink
Tacky	Cheap and Nasty
Taking the Mickey	Making fun of Someone
Tatty	Worn
Telly	Television
The House	Houses of Parliament, Westminster, London
The Smoke	London
The Sticks	In the Countryside
Tipple	Little Drink of Alcohol
Toff	Upper Class Gentleman
Toil	To Work hard
Totter	Street Trader
Twiggy	A 1960s fashion model
Twitten	Small Alley
Veg	Vegetables
Verbal	Verbal abuse
Wellies	Wellington Boots

This is a story that I have been writing for nearly four years now, I never seem to get the time to finish it. It is about a small fictitious village in the heart of East Sussex and the eccentric country folk who live there. Should I ever get arrested for multiple homicides and end up locked away for 30 years, then I promise to finish it. The first story in the series is the Summer Fayre, the most important day of the year in the village calendar and where all the villagers come together for one hilarious occasion. Enjoy the first chapter.

THE SUMMER FAYRE

Chapter One

With dawn approaching, Rea swooped off the weather vane of St. Marys Church. Silent as the fading stars in the heavens above, the barn owl swept over the village. Beneath her lay the assorted buildings of Shagwell-in-the-Field, all in a rough circle around the green, like a spider's web. Rea's yellow eyes, shining fire-bright, surveyed the land below, as her soft wings silently cut the summer air.

She made her way to Noggin's Barn, on the outskirts of the village. Quartering Knight's Field as she flew for the chance of a last meal before settling down for the day. The barn is where she spent many an hour hidden from prying eyes. It had stood, without foundations, for over two hundred years. A monument to a craftsman from the village of those days, Hugh Egbert.

The rising sun soon started to shorten the shadows over the village green, where the faded-white marquees stood, like Moorish tents, greeting the new day. Multicoloured bunting hung in the still air, waiting for a breeze to bring it to life.

All was quiet, save for the pattering of Scruffy, as he gnawed at one of the marquee ropes. The village badger's ancestors had always scampered this track across the green – long before man had taken up a stone and tied it to a stick to make a club. He was just annoyed that he had to move off his usual path and was taking it out on the rope.

Scruffy had no idea that today was the Summer Fayre.

With the scent of humans strong in his nostrils he soon shuffled off, leaving behind a trail in the dewy grass. He moved a little faster as the electric whine of the village milk float came to his ears. Ears that were bitten ragged from endless scuffles with local cats and dogs. Jake, the big bloodhound at 42 The Green, still limps from their brief but violent encounter last spring.

Phillip Daybrook, Jake's master, had chased Scruffy up the path with a garden broom, while Scruffy still had the hair of Jake's tail in his mouth.

Bernie was driving the milk float today just as he had been doing for over 15 years. Bernie loved his job, as he loved rather too many of the neighbouring women. Bernie was a local, born and bred. His schoolmaster Knobby Clarke wrote on his final school report: *Bernie has set himself low standards that he consistently fails to achieve.*

This had no effect on Bernie. He could not care less, for while the meaning of the word ambition failed to reveal itself to him, he had other assets that were appreciated around the area. Assets that were always in demand. Bernie was tall and dark. His natural olive skin was further bronzed by his outdoor life and the occasional trip to the leisure centre at Bexhill-on-Sea, where he could work out and then relax under the sun lamps.

The only thing that Bernie loved more than his women was himself. It was not his fault. It became apparent from an early age, that he had the gifts that nature endowed. Dark brown, brooding eyes that shot electric glances. Black hair that fell in short curls about his strong face, and a soft, deep voice that made women shiver.

Many summers past, a troop of Romanies had regularly stayed in Tenpenny Woods near the village. They would appear in late summer, working on the hop farms, picking throughout the autumn. Then, when all the work was finished, they would pack up and head for the port of Dover cross, and then work their way through Europe over the winter months. In early spring arriving back in the West Country to start their circuit all over.

They worked the dairy farms of Cornwall, then up to Nottingham. Down to

Norfolk for eed-work in the marshes, finishing the summer at the Kentish hop farms and vineyards of southeast England. Their route took them through many parts of the country, always coinciding with the season's work, bit planting, cultivating, stacking or harvesting.

It was a centuries-old tradition. Many farmers relied on their help at the busy times of year. Sadly their ways disappeared as modern farming methods and fast roads made their leisurely life impossible. The legacy they left on the land was from the more hot-blooded young men of the troop.

Bernie, though he never knew it, was one of the last of a kind. A midnight liaison in the freshly mown field on the edge of Shagwell, under a bright harvest moon, had produced a new life nearly three decades ago. In Bernie ran the ancient bloodline of the Romany Gypsy.

His forefathers had travelled from the Russian Steppes over eleven centuries before. A thousand years before that they had fled from Caesar's vanguard in Egypt and before that their original homelands in Northern India. They were a people destined to wander the earth until they were no more.

Bernie had morals of a sort. He never – well, almost never – messed around with married women. Although there were the odd occasions when his brain was put on the back-burner, overridden by pure lust. But he always treated them well and left them smiling. "All part of the service," he would say.

The stockbroker's wife was one of his exceptions and it could have ended in bloodshed. Crispian Fenton-Hardcrepe was from the old-school network. His father had arranged for his job on the London stock exchange two years before he left Eton. He boomed during the eighties, like so many in the *yuppie Thatcher* years, only to lose most of it on *Black Monday* from blatantly ignoring his father's words:

"Never gamble with what you cannot afford to lose."

His wife, Marilyn, was a beautiful accessory to his platinum credit card lifestyle. She lived life to the full, especially while her husband was away

for long hours of city work. Marilyn was a bitch in every sense of the word. Cunning but gracious all in one go. She was breathtakingly beautiful and attracted to money like a bee to nectar. She had the ability to look anyone straight in the eye whilst telling the biggest lies.

Marilyn had decided many years ago that money was her very favourite word. Men were mesmerised by her. Women disliked her on contact. On finding out about his money she had attached herself to Crispian and she had decided that he would do nicely, thank you. His apparently endless income was just about perfect.

On Black Monday, as stock markets crashed worldwide, Crispian saw most of his life's work vanish like water after a summer storm. He watched as one of his drunken colleagues leapt unsuccessfully from The Embankment, near Tower Bridge, in an effort to finish his shattered life. The fool landed at the river only to find that it was low tide. After a mud-bath and a change of clothes they then decided to take to drinking more seriously.

Crispian arrived home the next day, unannounced and still drunk. He was unaware of the commotion and panic he had caused in the master bedroom.

Bernie made his escape while Crispian was passing out in the drawing room of his mansion. His last words as he crashed to the floor with brandy glass held high, saluting his father's portrait, were: *"…we shall fight them on the beaches, we shall never, surrender!"* He lay there for 16 hours and remembered nothing. Marilyn made a bit of an effort by throwing the dog blanket over him. Since that time Bernie was much more careful about his romantic extra curricular activities.

All that seemed a distant dream now as Bernie's milk float whined its way past the green. Bottles clinking in the back. Bernie was idly whistling the tune *My old man's a dustman he wears a dustman's hat*, while slouching over his steering wheel. He stared lazily at the coloured flags around the Fayre. A big fabric sign, strung above the entrance, blazed out, SUMMER FAYRE TODAY in huge, hand-painted, red letters, all welcome rain or shine.

…To be continued…

Well, that's it the first of the Random Threads trilogy all done and dusted. I do hope you enjoyed my ramblings. Who could ever believe that fixing sewing machines could be so much fun!

A few of my favourite remarks about the trilogy

(Amazingly there are another 30 pages of them on my website received from all over the globe.)

You'll be back for more – Country Life

Evocative and descriptive. Excellent writing – Professor Jacque Johnson

Wonderful warm and charming. Alex has a remarkable talent – Anne Brennan: President Allegro Communications.

Alex's books are rare, desired and most welcome – Capt R. Wightman

A trilogy of local gems – Aspect County Magazine.

You will be entranced by his stories and travels around Sussex – Sussex Books.

A well polished masterpiece – What's On Magazine

You may feel that you know Sussex but I guarantee Alex will make you look again and fill your minds with the happiest of thoughts – Frank Scutt OBE

I retired to my bed, and let your book give me a glimpse of somewhere else, through the eyes of someone else, by the time I turned off my reading light, I was at peace with the world. Not convinced it is either safe or sane, but the edge softened by your beautiful words. – Pat Bergman, USA

I couldn't put it down, Hillaire Belloc would have been happy to put his name to a book like this – John Allen, Magnet Magazine

Word pictures of landscapes and pictures straight from the heart. A fascinating read – Jim Flegg, Country Ways Television

full of laughter, even a few tears, folklore and wisdom. Books to be dipped into and treasured a delightful trilogy – The Hash

As this is the revised second edition of Vol I, I have the ability to see the future and let you know the ISBN numbers and titles of the next two in the trilogy.

Random Threads Vol II Skylark Country ISBN 0-9539410-2-7

Random Thread Vol III High Street & Hedgerows ISBN 0-9539410-3-5

For more information email me @ alexsussex@aol.com

or visit:

www.sussexsewingmachines.com

www.crowsnestpublications.com

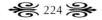

224